Up and
Using Creative and Critical Thinking Skills to Enhance Learning

Andrew P. Johnson
Minnesota State University, Mankato

Allyn and Bacon
Boston London Toronto Sydney Tokyo Singapore

To the hardworking teachers and staff in Grantsburg, Wisconsin.

ISBN 0-205-29731-5

Printed in the United States of America

10 9 8 7 6 5 4 3 2 1   03 02 01 00 99

Contents

Preface

When I first started teaching second grade in River Falls, Wisconsin, back in 1983, I heard a lot about high level thinking, critical thinking, and thinking skills. I knew these were important and they should be included in my classroom, but I was never really sure exactly what they were and how I was to go about teaching them. The purpose of this book is to bridge the gap between theory and practice and in turn, enhance the pedagogical skills and practice of classroom teachers. Specific goals related to this are to: (a) define thinking skills and their purpose; (b) describe the theory upon which thinking skills are based; (c) outline effective thinking skills instruction; and (d) demonstrate how thinking skills can be used to enhance classroom practice in all curriculum areas and at all levels.

1

What Are Thinking Skills?

Learning how to use thinking skills is not as complicated as some would have you believe. Once learned, thinking skills can be readily applied to daily lessons in all curriculum areas to enhance learning. This chapter begins the journey by examining (a) the value of thinking, (b) intelligence, (c) the information processing model, and (d) a definition of thinking skills.

EFFECTIVE THINKING IS VALUED

While our knowledge about subjects can change, fade, or become obsolete, our ability to think effectively remains constant. Effective thinking strategies allow us to acquire the necessary knowledge and apply it appropriately. Effective thinking is a trait valued in theory by schools at all levels; however, it is something which is rarely given a great deal of attention in practice (Gardner, 1991). Research indicates that while levels of basic skills have remained consistent or shown a slight increase, students are not acquiring effective thinking strategies (Mullis & Jenkins, 1990). Indeed, knowledge of instructional strategies used in developing higher order thinking has had minimal impact on the way students are taught in classrooms, with the transmission of knowledge still the predominant model used in teaching (Armour-Thomas & Allen, 1993).

If students are to learn higher and more complex ways of thinking, and if we are to move beyond knowledge-transmission models of teaching, it makes sense that thinking skills instruction be examined as a potential tool to use in enhancing the curriculum. In other words, if we want students to be proficient thinkers, we must teach them how.

COMPONENTS OF INTELLIGENCE

A common goal of education is to develop intelligent, well-informed citizens. Perkins (1986) has developed an equation describing intelligence as consisting of three components: power, knowledge, and tactics (intelligence will

1

be explored more thoroughly in Chapter 5). Here, each of these is described in turn.

Power

Power in Perkins' sense can be thought of as innate cognitive capacity, a trait which includes attention, will, perception, and plasticity of the nervous system (Sternberg, 1990). This part of Perkins' equation represents one's level of mental energy or cognitive power which is an inherent trait with a limited capacity for improvement.

Using a computer analogy here, cognitive power could be compared to the amount of memory on your hard drive and on your desktop working space. Does your computer have 4K or 36K of RAM? Is it an old Apple IIc? A 286 PC? Or a Pentium? This affects the kind and amount of programs you can run and the speed at which they operate. With computers, however, extra chips can be inserted to increase the power. Humans must make due with what they have.

Knowledge

Knowledge, the second component in Perkins' equation, is generally seen as an essential part of being educated, and is an integral component of intelligent behavior. Bereiter and Scardamalia (1992) explain that background knowledge is used to lessen the cognitive demands of problem solving, to guide perception, and to organize and encode new information. Research has shown knowledge to positively affect perception (Chase & Simon, 1973), categorization and problem-solving (Chi, Feltovich, & Glaser, 1981), general learning (Bereiter & Scardamalia, 1992), reading comprehension (Goodman, 1986; Smith, 1985), and memory (Recht & Leslie, 1988). However, most theorists believe that while knowledge is necessary for education and thinking of any kind, it is not sufficient (Resnick & Klopfer, 1989). Simply supplying students with information does not provide them with a very interesting way to learn; nor is it an effective approach to teaching, as it has a tendency to produce knowledge which lies inert or unused (Perkins & Salomon, 1989; Swartz, 1991).

Using the computer analogy again, knowledge could be compared to the number and kind of programs you might have on your hard drive. Each of these programs contains vast amounts of information which enhance the power and utility of a computer.

Tactics

Tactics, the third component of Perkins' equation, are the cognitive strategies or thinking skills learners employ to more effectively use both the power and knowledge components. The premise of thinking skills instruction is that effective ways of thinking can be taught and internalized, and this premise has a good deal of empirical support. Research indicates that thinking skills instruction can improve students' mastery of content and performance (Mahn & Greenwood, 1990; Zohar & Tamir, 1993; Zohar, Weinberger, & Tamir, 1994), and enhance reasoning capabilities and higher level thinking (Hoskyns, Cook, Quellmalz, & Mundform, 1993; Zohar et al., 1994).

Staying with the computer analogy, tactics could be compared to the strategies a human uses to operate a computer program. Data bases, word processing programs, and vast amounts of computer memory are all useless without humans who have the skills to use and apply them.

INFORMATION PROCESSING MODEL

Cognitive psychology examines how humans process the world around them. This information processing model below illustrates how learning takes place (see Figure 1.1). As new information is perceived, it is stored in short term memory (STM). STM has a very limited capacity, holding about seven chunks of information for approximately 15 seconds (Miller, 1956). It is here that the new information is processed and eventually stored in long term memory (LTM). LTM is like a gigantic file cabinet in our heads holding a tremendous amount of information for an unlimited amount of time.

Using yet another computer analogy: perception would be the input from the keyboard, STM would be the amount of RAM on the desktop working space, and LTM would be the amount of ROM on the computer hard drive.

With human information processing systems, information flows two ways: First, it flows from perception, to STM where it is processed, then to LTM where it is stored. But information also flows the other way. Information stored in LTM is used to process information in STM and also to help humans perceive patterns or attend to important information around them. This two-way flow of information is know as the interactive model (Graves, Juel, & Graves, 1998). This means that humans use the information in their heads together with information perceived in the environment to help create or construct meaning.

THINKING SKILLS

A thinking skill is a cognitive process broken down into a set of explicit steps which are then used to guide thinking (Johnson, 1996; Perkins, 1986). Thinking skills allow one's cognitive system to function more efficiently. Thorough teaching here allows the learner to achieve automaticity in the various cognitive processes. This decreases the demands placed on STM, thereby increasing the cognitive space available for further learning or other kinds of thinking (Bereiter & Scardamalia, 1992). Schneider and Shiffrin (1977), in their work with information processing systems, demonstrate that cognitive processes which have become automated place far less demand on the learner's cognitive

Figure 1.1 Information Processing Model

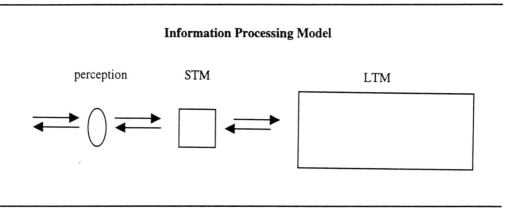

Information Processing Model

perception   STM   LTM

resources than those cognitive processes which must be controlled. One goal of thinking skills instruction, therefore, is to learn thinking skills to the point of automaticity, thus allowing the learner to focus on meaning, engage in higher levels of thinking, access relevant knowledge more readily, and process and sort incoming information more efficiently (Bereiter & Scardamalia, 1992).

A second goal of thinking skills instruction is to develop competent thinkers and problem solvers. This is accomplished by providing learners with a repertoire of skills that can be used to meet the demands of various tasks and situations. These skills are most readily learned by making cognitive processes clear and providing explicit instruction (Armour-Thomas & Allen, 1993; Bereiter & Scardamalia, 1992).

Thinking Skills Versus High Level and Critical Thinking

Is high level thinking the same as a thinking skill? No. High level thinking is any cognitive operation which is complex or places high demands on the processing taking place in short term memory. Students do not benefit from being exposed to high level thinking tasks unless there is explicit instruction first. For example, a teacher could ask students to compare and contrast the Wicked Witch in the Wizard of Oz to Darth Vadar in Star Wars. Students who are already fairly adept at high level thinking will be able to do this while other students will probably become frustrated. Unfortunately, this is what often happens under the guise of developing high level thinking: Teachers simply present high level tasks. However, no teaching and very little learning take place in these situations.

Thinking skills instruction, on the other hand, makes learning this cognitive process fairly simple: If you want students to be able to compare and contrast, you must first break the cognitive process into steps: (a) Look at the whole, (b) find the similarities, (c) find the differences, and (d) describe. This operation is then taught using explicit instruction. With appropriate instruction, high level thinking becomes relatively easy. This idea is the underlying premise of this book: Complicated things are made easy by breaking them into parts and teaching them. Good teachers are able to break complicated skills and concepts down into their component parts so that their students can understand and learn.

A thinking skill is like a skill found in athletics, music, dance, art, or any other area. In order to teach it effectively, it must be broken down into steps so that it can be taught. For example, if I wanted to teach my friend Kathryn how to serve in the game of racquetball, I could simply give her a racquet, give her an opponent, and push her into the court. This would be a high level skill that Kathryn would find very challenging. A good athlete would eventually be able to grasp the skills needed to serve effectively; however, Kathyrn and most others would become frustrated long before they learned how to serve. But, if I broke the serve into steps and walked Kathryn through the steps several times, she would learn to serve more quickly and more effectively with a minimal amount of frustration. Eventually, she would not have to think about the steps and could concentrate on where to put the ball and other serving strategies.

Is critical thinking the same as a thinking skill? No. Critical thinking is a type of thinking where a person must organize, analyze, or evaluate given information. However, each of these operations could become a thinking skill if it were broken into parts and taught explicitly (Chapter 5 will provide a more thorough examination of this).

General and Domain-Specific Thinking Skills

There are two types of thinking skills which might be taught: general and domain-specific (Bruer, 1993). General thinking skills are generic cognitive processes which can be used in many subjects or settings such as comparing and contrasting. Domain-specific thinking skills are specific cognitive processes which are used in particular subjects or settings such as mathematical algorithms. This book will focus on general thinking skills. General thinking skills are described by many as having the most value in an instructional setting as they are more easily learned and applicable to many subjects and settings (Marzano, 1991; Smagorinsky, 1991).

Thinking Frames

In teaching thinking skills it is important to have a method to initially guide students' thinking. A thinking frame can be used here (Johnson, 1998; Perkins, 1987). A thinking frame is a concrete representation of a particular cognitive process broken down into specific steps and used to support the thought process. Thinking frames can be effectively constructed in poster form and placed in the classroom for teaching and easy review. An example of a thinking frame for comparing and contrasting can be seen in Figure 1. 2.

Figure 1.2 Example of a Thinking Frame

Comparing and Contrasting: Given two or more items, the student will find their similarities and differences.
  Thinking Frame
  A. Look at all items.
  B. Find the similarities.
  C. Find the differences.
  D. Describe.

Up and Out

This book describes nineteen thinking skills and the corresponding thinking frames and illustrates how they might be used throughout the curriculum. This is not meant to be an exhaustive list. A thinking skill is any cognitive process broken into steps. Thus, after reading this book you will be able to add some of your own to this list based on those cognitive processes you perceive to be important.

SUMMARY

1. The ability to think is valued; however, ways of thinking must be taught.
2. Intelligence is made up of cognitive power, knowledge, and tactics or thinking skills.
3. The information processing model can be used to understand learning processes and thinking skills.
4. A thinking skill is any cognitive process broken down into steps.
5. Learning how to use thinking skills allows one's cognitive system to function more efficiently.
6. Thinking skills are different than high level thinking.
7. Thinking skills can be general or domain-specific.
8. Thinking frames are the concrete representation of a cognitive process broken down into steps which are used to support the thinking process.

References

Armour-Thomas, E., & Allen, B. (1993). How well do teachers teach for the promotion of student thinking and learning. Educational Horizons, 71, 203-208.

Bereiter, C., & Scardamalia, M. (1992). Cognition in curriculum. In P.W. Jackson (Ed.), Handbook of research on curriculum (pp. 517-542). New York: American Educational Research Association.

Bruer, J.T. (1993). Schools for thought. Cambridge, MA: MIT Press.

Chase, W.G., & Simon, H.A. (1973). Perceptions in chess. Cognitive Psychology, 4, 55-81.

Chi, M.T., Feltovich, P.J., & Glaser, R. (1981). Categorization and representation of physics problems by experts and novices. Cognitive Science, 5, 121-152.

Gardner, H. (1991). The unschooled mind: How children think and how schools should teach them. New York: Harper Collins.

Goodman, K. (1986). What's whole in whole language? Portsmouth, NH: Heinemann.

Graves, M., Juel, C., & Graves, B. (1998). Teaching reading for the 21st century. Needham Heights, MA: Allyn and Bacon.

Hoskyn, J., Cook N.R., Quellmalz, E.S., & Mundform, D. (1993). Multicultural Reading and Thinking Program (McRAT). Atlanta, GA: American Educational Research Association. (ERIC Document Reproduction Service No. ED 358 432).

Johnson, A. (1998). Word class: A way to modify spelling instruction for gifted learners, The Roeper Review, 20, 128-131.

Johnson, A. (1996). Inference: A thinking skill to enhance learning and literacy. WSRA Journal, 40, 9-13.

Mahn, C., & Greenwood, G. (1990). Cognitive behavior modification: Use of self-instruction by first graders on academic tasks. Journal of Educational Research, 83, 158-161.

Marzano, R. (1991). Tactics for thinking: A program for initiating the teaching of thinking. In A. Costa (Ed.), Developing minds (Vol. 2) (pp. 65-68). Alexandria, VI: Association of Supervision and Curriculum Development.

Miller, G.A. (1956). The magical number seven, plus or minus two: Some limits on our capacity for processing information. Psychological Review, 63, 81-97.

Mullis, I.V., & Jenkins, L.B. (1990). The reading report card. 1971-1988: Trends from the nation's report card. Princeton, NJ: National Assessment of Educational Progress, Educational Testing Service.

Perkins. D.N. (1986). Thinking frames. Educational Leadership, 42, 4-10.

Perkins, D.N. (1987). Thinking frames: An integrative perspective on teaching cognitive skills. In J.B. Baron & R.J. Sternberg (Eds.), Teaching thinking skills: Theory and practice (pp. 41-61). New York: W.H. Freeman.

Perkins, D.N., & Salomon, G. (1989). Are cognitive skills context bound? Educational Researcher, 47, 16-25.

Recht, D.R., & Leslie, L. (1988). Effect of prior knowledge on good and poor readers' memory. Journal of Educational Psychology, 80, 16-20.

Resnick, L.B., & Klopfer, L.E. (1989) Toward the thinking curriculum: An overview. In L.B. Resnick & E. Klopfer (Eds.), Toward the thinking curriculum (pp. 1-18). Washington, DC: Association for Supervision and Curriculum Development.

Schneider, W., & Shiffrin, R. (1977). Controlled and automatic human information processing: Detection, search and attention. Psychological Review, 84, 1-66.

Smith, F. (1985). Reading without nonsense (2nd ed.). New York: Teachers College Press.

Smagorinsky, P. (1991). The writer's knowledge and the writing process: A protocol analysis. Research in the Teaching of English, 25, 339-363.

Sternberg, R. (1990). Metaphors of mind: Conceptions of the nature of intelligence. New York: Press Syndicate of the University of Cambridge.

Swartz, R. (1991) Infusing the teaching of critical thinking into content instruction. In A. Costa (Ed.), Developing minds (pp. 177-184). Alexandria, VA: Association of Supervision and Curriculum Development.

Zohar, A., & Tamir, P. (1993). Incorporating critical thinking into a regular high school biology curriculum. School Science and Mathematics, 93, 136-140.

Zohar, A., Weinberger, Y., & Tamir, P. (1994). The effect of the biology critical thinking project on the development of critical thinking. Journal of Research in Science Teaching, 31, 183-196.

2

The Basics of Thinking Skills

This chapter describes four areas related to thinking skills instruction: (a) approaches to thinking skills instruction, (b) acquisition and transfer of thinking skills, (c) thinking skills and academic achievement, and (d) using thinking skills to enhance classroom instruction.

APPROACHES TO THINKING SKILLS INSTRUCTION

How should thinking skills be taught? There are three approaches used in teaching thinking skills: the stand-alone approach, the immersion approach, and the embedded approach (Prawat, 1991).

The Stand-Alone Approach

The stand-alone approach consists of teaching thinking skills separately from subject-matter content (see Figure 2.1). Here a general set of thinking skills are identified and taught as a separate course or subject. Students are instructed how to transfer the skills to various subjects and situations. The problem with this approach is that students do not have a context in which to learn and use acquired skills. The skills are viewed as puzzles with little relevance to academic or real life tasks. Also, thinking skills learned in isolation do not transfer well to academic or real world situations (Graves, 1983; Perkins & Salomon, 1989).

To again use the analogy of my friend Kathryn learning to play racquetball: this would be like learning and practicing assorted racquetball skills outside the racquetball court without ever playing a game. It would be hard for Kathryn to see the relevance of each skill and there is no reason to assume that when she finally got onto the court to play, she would know how and when to use all the skills that she had spent time learning.

If a classroom teacher were to use this approach to the teaching of thinking skills, students would spend a great deal of time looking at a series of puzzles, word problems, or exercises presented in a book. It would be assumed that students would be able to transfer these skills to other situations. However, this would happen in only a few instances.

The Immersion Approach

The immersion approach does not involve teaching thinking skills; rather, it allows good thinking to develop naturally as a result of students being fully engaged or immersed in content-related activities which call for high levels of thinking. Here, students are provided with repeated practice in complex cognitive activities with the assumption that they will eventually develop the necessary cognitive skills to successfully engage in high level thinking. As stated in the previous chapter, simply immersing students in high level thinking activities is not an effective teaching and learning technique: High ability students reinforce those ways of thinking already acquired while other students become frustrated. A series of challenging questions and activities is not a thinking skills program.

Again, this would be like giving Kathryn a racquet and a ball, and pushing her on to the court to play. She would eventually pick up a random assortment of skills; however, she would not learn them very fast and there is a good chance that frustration would impede much of her learning and her desire to play. Most would agree that simply immersing students in a task without instruction is not a very effective way to learn any kind of skill.

If a classroom teacher were to use this approach to the teaching of thinking skills, students would be assigned complex tasks. It would be assumed here that over time, students would be able to discover the steps necessary to complete these complex tasks and develop the appropriate thinking skills. Again, this would happen in only a few instances.

The Embedded Approach

The embedded approach teaches thinking skills within a subject matter context. Here, thinking skills are taught in science, social studies, language arts, or some other subject. Students then apply these skills directly to the particular subject matter being studied. This allows students to use the skills in a meaningful context and helps them learn the subject matter more deeply. An embedded approach is recommended here as being the most effective way to teach thinking skills. Rather than an additional subject, thinking skills should be used to enhance whatever curriculum is currently being taught.

Using the embedded approach, we would get Kathryn on the racquetball court first, then while playing the game, she would be taught one or two skills each session. The skills would be taught in short lessons either before, during, or after each game so that she could apply them directly. Through extensive playing and brief instruction, Kathryn would eventually master each skill. Skills here are seen as a means to an end, not an end in and of themselves. Mastery is not expected initially; rather, it is realized over time through repeated practice and exposure.

Using this approach, a classroom teacher would teach thinking skills as part of a reading, science, or social studies class. Using direct instruction, modeling, and guided practice, the teacher would go over the specific steps of this skill. Students would then be asked to apply this skill to some aspect of the lesson.

Figure 2.1 Approaches to Thinking Skills Instruction

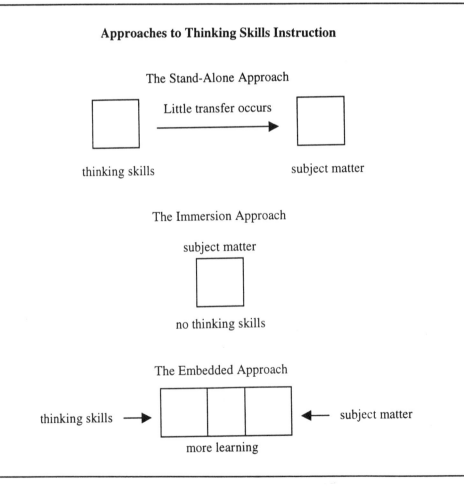

Approaches to Thinking Skills Instruction

The Stand-Alone Approach

Little transfer occurs

thinking skills   subject matter

The Immersion Approach

subject matter

no thinking skills

The Embedded Approach

thinking skills →   ← subject matter

more learning

ACQUISITION AND TRANSFER OF
THINKING SKILLS INSTRUCTION

How might a student best acquire a skill initially? Lesson planning and the elements of effective skills instruction will be covered more thoroughly in Chapter 3; however, a brief overview is useful here. Perkins (1986) describes three elements of instruction in this regard: acquisition, internalization, and transfer. These elements ensure that students not only acquire the skill, but are then able to apply it in other settings and situations.

Acquisition includes direct instruction, modeling, guided practice, and individual practice. The first and most important part of acquiring a thinking skill is direct instruction. A review of research indicates that students appear to benefit whenever cognitive processes or strategies are made clear and explicit (Adams, 1989; Bereiter & Scardamalia, 1992; Chance, 1986; Collins, Brown, & Neuman, 1989; Marzano, 1991).

Internalization includes practicing the application of the thinking skill so that it becomes automatic. Automaticity is the condition whereby a learner is able to apply a skill with little conscious effort (Laberge & Samuels, 1974). Automaticity of a thinking skill is achieved through guided practice and repetition (Bereiter & Scardamalia, 1992; Bransford & Vye, 1989). Bransford and Vye state that expert performance in any area relies on the automaticity of relevant cognitive processes. This allows the performer to expend a minimum of cognitive capacity on the process and more capacity concentrating on the finished product.

Transfer occurs when the learner is able to use a thinking skill beyond the particular teaching/learning context. For thinking skills to have any value, transfer must occur. Perkins and Salomon (1988) identify two types of transfer: low-road transfer and high-road transfer.

Low-road transfer occurs when there is an automatic triggering of well-practiced routines in similar contexts or situations. Here, the skill is taught along with particular applications in varied contexts using what Perkins and Salomon (1988) refer to as hugging. Extensive practice of the thinking skill in specific situations leads to automaticity. Students respond to particular stimuli as they become able to apply the skill to perceptually similar situations.

High-road transfer occurs when the guiding principles of the skill have been grasped by the learner so that it can be applied and adapted to other contexts or situations. Here, the goals of a particular skill are taught using what Perkins and Salomon refer to as bridging (1988). Using bridging as a technique, a teacher might well ask, "What thinking skill would work best here? How might we use this thinking skill? Where would you use this skill in your school life? Or, where do you see yourself using this skill in your life outside of school?" The learner is eventually able to apply this skill to other contexts or situations.

There is, however, considerable disagreement as to whether or not transfer occurs at all, under what conditions, and to what extent (Bransford, Sherwood, Vye, & Rieser, 1986; Dudly-Marling & Owston, 1988; Gick & Holyoak, 1983; Klauer, 1989; Niedelman, 1991; Norris, 1985). Perkins and Salomon (1988) believe that transfer does occur if hugging and bridging are consistently taught. However, if embedded approach to thinking skills instruction is used, the issue of transfer becomes less important.

THINKING SKILLS AND ACADEMIC ACHIEVEMENT

Thinking skills instruction seems to have a positive effect on learning, possibly because students are processing information at deeper levels (Craik & Lockhart, 1972), and thus avoiding the problem of inert knowledge as described by Bransford and Nye (1989). That is, knowledge that is not used or applied becomes static in LTM, making it harder to access or retrieve. Infusing thinking skills into a curriculum allows students to manipulate new ideas, make more connections to other things, and thus learn more deeply (Marzano, 1991).

Teaching thinking skills can affect knowledge acquisition (Collins, 1991; Crow & Haws, 1985; Worhsam & Austin, 1983; Zohar, Weinberger, & Tamir, 1994). Prawat (1991) describes learning and understanding as the very goals of thinking skills instruction. Glaser (1984) states that there is an unavoidable interaction between structures of knowledge and cognitive processes. Having a body of knowledge affects one's thinking and at the same time, thinking affects one's procurement, understanding, and application of knowledge.

USING THINKING SKILLS TO ENHANCE
CLASSROOM INSTRUCTION

There are five ways in which thinking skills can be used to enhance classroom instruction: First, thinking skills can be used to prepare students for learning by generating ideas and activating relevant schemata. This makes it more likely that they will connect new knowledge to known knowledge.

Second, thinking skills can be used to help students organize ideas. Part of being human is having the need to bring order to the world around us. We search for meaningful patterns, organize information, and put things in groups or categories in order to understand. This is evidenced most clearly in science where objects, concepts, or events are analyzed and put into phylum, categories, or classifications.

Third, thinking skills can be used to help students see the structure of an object, concept, or an event. Knowing the structure, students are better able to understand its parts.

Fourth, thinking skills can be used to help students establish relationships between two or more objects, concepts, or events. Focusing on similarities and differences helps to build bridges between prior knowledge and new knowledge. Wittrock (1990) asserts that learning with real understanding occurs only when the learner is able to generate meaningful relationships between the known and the unknown. Perkins (1991) advocates a curriculum that encourages connection-making in order to develop understanding and insight.

And finally, understanding thinking skills and knowing how to use the thinking skills described in this book will provide a teacher with a vast repertoire of activities to use with any unit or lesson. Instead of relying on textbooks and teaching manuals, teachers will be able to use thinking skills to creatively design their own learning experiences.

SUMMARY

1. Thinking skills instruction should be embedded within the current curriculum.
2. Direct instruction, modeling, guided practice, and individual practices will help students learn thinking skills and transfer them to other situations.
3. Thinking skills can be used to help students learn more and learn more deeply.
4. Teachers can use thinking skills to design activities and enhance classroom instruction.

References

Adams, M.J. (1989). Thinking skills curricula: Their promise and progress. Educational Psychologist, 24, 24-77.

Bereiter, C., & Scardamalia, M. (1992). Cognition in curriculum. In P.W. Jackson (Ed.), Handbook of research on curriculum (pp. 517-542). New York: American Educational Research Association.

Beyer, B.K. (1984). Improving thinking skills: Practical approaches. Phi Delta Kappan, 65, 556-560.

Bransford, J.D., Sherwood, R.D., Vye, N.J., & Rieser, J. (1986), Teaching thinking and problem solving: Research foundations. American Psychologist, 41, 1078-1089.

Bransford, J.D., & Vye, N.J. (1989). A perspective on cognitive research and its implications for instruction. In L.B. Resnick & L.E. Klopfer (Eds.), Toward the thinking curriculum (pp. 88-102). Washington, DC: Association for Supervision and Curriculum Development.

Chance, P. (1986). Thinking in the classroom. New York: Teachers College Press.

Collins, A., Brown, J.S., & Neuman, S. (1989). Cognitive apprenticeship: Teaching the crafts of reading, writing and mathematics. In L.B. Resnick (Ed.), Knowing, learning, and instruction: Essays in honor of Robert Glaser (pp. 453-494). Hillsdale, NJ: Erlbaum.

Collins, C. (1991). Reading instruction that increases thinking ability. Journal of Reading, 34, 510-516.

Craik, F.I.M., & Lockhart, R.S. (1972). Levels of processing: Framework for memory research. Journal of Verbal Learning and Verbal Behavior, 11, 671-684.

Crow, L.W., & Haws, S.G. (1985). The effects of teaching reasoning upon students' critical thinking and science achievement. French Lick Springs, IN: National Association for Research in Science Teaching. (ERIC Document Reproduction Service No. ED 255 371).

Dudley-Marling, C., & Owston, R.D. (1988). Using computers to teach problem solving: A critical review. Educational Technology, 26, 27-33.

Gick, M.L., & Holyoak, K.J. (1983). Schema induction and analogical transfer. Cognitive Psychology, 15, 1-38.

Glaser, R. (1984). Education and thinking: The role of knowledge. American Psychologist, 39, 93-104.

Graves, D. (1983). Writing: Teacher and children at work. Portsmouth, NH: Heinemann.

Klauer, K. (1989). Teaching for analogical transfer as a means of improving problem-solving, thinking and learning. Instructional Science, 18, 179-192.

LaBerge, D., & Samuels, S.J. (1974). Toward a theory of automatic information processing in reading. Cognitive Psychology, 6, 283-323.

Marzano, R. (1991). Tactics for thinking: A program for initiating the teaching of thinking. In A. Costa (Ed.), Developing minds (Vol. 2) (pp. 65-68). Alexandria, VI: Association of Supervision and Curriculum Development.

Niedelman, M. (1991). Problem solving and transfer. Journal of Learning Disabilities, 24, 322-329.

Norris, S. (1985). Synthesis of research on critical thinking. Educational Leadership, 42, 40-45.

Perkins. D.N. (1986). Thinking frames. Educational Leadership, 42, 4-10.

Perkins, D.N. (1991). Educating for insight. Educational Leadership, 43, 4-8.

Perkins, D.N., & Salomon, G. (1988). Teaching for transfer. Educational Leadership, 46, 22-32.

Perkins, D.N., & Salomon, G. (1989). Are cognitive skills context bound? Educational Researcher, 47, 16-25.

Prawat, R. (1991). Embedded thinking skill instruction in subject matter instruction. In A. Costa (Ed.), Developing minds (Vol. 1), (pp. 185-186). Alexandria, VI: Association of Supervision and Curriculum Development.

Prawat, R. (1991). The value of ideas: The immersion approach to the development of thinking. Educational Researcher, 20, 3-10.

Wittrock, M. (1990). Students' thought processes. In M. Wittrock (Ed.), Handbook of research on teaching (3rd ed.) (pp. 297-314).

Worsham, A. & Austin, G. (1983). Effects of teaching thinking skills on SAT scores. Educational Leadership, 39, 50-51.

Zohar, A., Weinberger, Y., & Tamir, P. (1994). The effect of the biology critical thinking project on the development of critical thinking. Journal of Research in Science Teaching, 31 (2), 183-196.

3

Teaching Thinking Skills

Thinking skills will be of little use if they are not taught in a manner in which students can understand and learn to use them. This chapter includes (a) a description of lesson plans and (b) the elements of effective instruction as they relate to thinking skills instruction.

LESSON PLANS

Good teaching does not happen by accident; it must be planned. Thoughtful planning links the curriculum to the particulars of instruction, allowing for more purposeful instruction, and enhancing the possibility of effective lessons (Clark & Dunn, 1991; Freiberg & Driscoll, 1992; Parker & Jarolimek, 1997). Thoughtful planning also helps the teacher understand the content of the lesson (Clark & Dunn, 1991), create a logical sequence of instructional events (Clark & Peterson, 1986; Freiberg & Driscoll, 1992), and connect activities to instructional objectives (Parker & Jarolimek, 1997).

Effective lesson plans enhance learning by increasing time on-task (Clark & Peterson, 1986; Freiberg & Driscoll, 1992; Stringfield & Teddlie, 1991), and helping students to perceive the structure of new information so that it can be more easily assimilated (Freiberg & Driscoll, 1992; Walberg, 1991). Thoughtful planning makes teachers better able to incorporate new instructional strategies, utilize more complex learning activities (Freiberg & Driscoll, 1992), and to feel more confident and less uncertain during instruction (Clark & Dunn, 1991; Clark & Peterson, 1986; Freiberg & Driscoll, 1992). Lesson design also affects classroom management by reducing chaos, guiding the flow of events, and keeping students interested and engaged (Freiberg & Driscoll, 1992).

However, planning a lesson is a complex endeavor consisting of many problems to be solved: What is the objective? Why is this worth teaching? What exactly should students know or be able to do? How should information be organized so that students can understand? How much information should be given to them? What kind of activity should be designed to help students manipulate ideas presented? Lesson planning is a cognitive process that can be broken down into steps which, if followed, make this complex endeavor easier and more effective. In this sense, lesson planning is very much like a thinking skill. And just like thinking skills, this process becomes internalized through practice and repetition.

Lesson Plan Form

What are the steps of effective lesson planning? Madeline Hunter (1984) suggests that effective lessons should contain the following eight elements: (a) anticipatory set, (b) objective and purpose, (c) input, (d) modeling, (e) checking for understanding, (f) guided practice, (g) independent practice, and (h) closure. However, this form is cumbersome and may not be practical for every teaching situation. Instead, the lesson plan form in Figure 3.1 presents a modified version which is descriptive enough to be useful, yet flexible enough to be used. This form can be thought of as a type of thinking frame used to guide teachers' thinking as learning experiences are being planned. It allows the teacher to organize what is to be taught and helps in designing meaningful activities.

Figure 3.1 Lesson Plan Format

JOHNSON LESSON PLAN FORMAT

Teacher: _____ Grade: _____

Subject: _____ Time: _____

I. OBJECTIVE:

II. INTRODUCTION:

III. INPUT AND ACTIVITIES:

IV. CLOSURE

* Use the back side for lesson reflection. What worked well? What surprised you? What would you do differently?

Lesson Plan Parts

When designing a lesson, start with a specific objective. Make sure the lesson is complete, descriptive, and sequential with all questions and activities clearly explained. The rule of thumb is that a substitute teacher should be able to pick up the lesson plan and teach the lesson. Listed here are a basic set of lesson plans parts which can be used flexibly to construct any type of lesson.

1. Objective. This is a definition of what students should know or be able to do as a result of instruction. This is where the planning process begins. What is it exactly that you want to teach? There is generally one objective for each lesson and it should be stated in simple terms. Behavioral objectives need not, and in most instances, should not be used. Behaviorally stated objectives have their roots in behavioral psychology and are not consistent with a cognitive approach to learning (Tobin & Fraser, 1991). A strict reliance on behavioral objectives also implies that learning is a finite endeavor when in fact it is a dynamic interaction between known and new information. Finally, behavioral objectives are not pragmatic, they complicate the lesson planning process, and they place less emphasis on a constructivist approach to learning.

Lesson objectives should sound a good deal like students describing what they learned in school to their parents. For example, a student is more apt to say, "I learned about frog eggs," rather than, "I demonstrated my knowledge of frog eggs by designing a chart which compared frog eggs to the eggs of five other animals." Keep it simple.

In the same vein, describing an activity is not the same as an objective. For example, "The students will create a chart comparing frogs to toads," would not be an objective. While this is a very interesting activity, it simply describes what students will be doing but not the information needed or the purpose for doing it. An appropriate objective instead might be, "Students will learn the differences between frogs and toads." The chart comparing frogs to toads would be an activity used towards this end.

2. Introduction. This is a quick way to introduce students to the concepts or ideas found in the lesson. An introduction links new ideas to known ideas, arouses curiosity and creates interests. These are relatively brief (one to three minutes), and are usually written last.

3. Input. Learning involves the construction of knowledge as new information is given meaning in terms of prior knowledge (Tobin & Fraser, 1991). Whether it be concepts or skills, all learning requires some sort of information. Discovery learning or inquiry is not an excuse for learning-by-guessing exercises. All activities need to be set in a knowledge-based context. Here, the teacher organizes and lists in outline form exactly what is to be taught. Questions for students should be recorded here. If a skill is being taught, the steps should be written out in sequence. All information here must directly support the lesson objective.

4. *Activity*. This involves the manipulation of the input. Older students may be able to use more abstract activities to manipulate the input, although this is generally not the preferred method. Younger students need to physically manipulate or interact with the input in some fashion. Examples include: creative writing, drawing, simulation, discussion, problem solving, drama, graphing, worksheets, games, experiments, homework assignments, or thinking skills.

5. *Closure/Review*. This element varies depending on the type of lesson. It is generally a short review of the main ideas covered in a lesson and sometimes a preview of the next day's lesson; however, many lessons do not contain this element.

Evaluation

Evaluation is not a part of the lesson plan format here. It is assumed that teachers will be using formative evaluation to observe learning as it happens and will monitor and adjust accordingly.

Sample Lesson Plan

Figure 3.2 depicts a sample lesson plan designed according to this format. Note that the information is presented in outline form using short, abbreviated sentences. The purpose of the lesson plan is to organize thinking during planning and to provide a guide during implementation. Notice also that the teacher here includes notes to himself in parentheses which, among other things, tell when to present visual aids.

Criteria for Lesson Plans

Included here are a set of criteria which can be used to enhance the designing of lesson plans (Figure 3.3). This is a quick and easy way for teacher educators to provide specific feedback relative to each part of a lesson plan. This also provides a structure so that preservice teachers can reflect on their own lessons or give feedback to others. Finally, these criteria provide the experienced teachers with an instrument to use in reflecting on specific learning experiences.

Figure 3.2 Sample Lesson Plan

Teacher: Andrew Johnson   Grade: 2
Subject: Science   Time: 1:50 - 2:50

OBJECTIVE: Students will learn about dinosaurs (general overview).

INTRODUCTION: Today we're going to learn about some huge animals that lived long ago: dinosaurs.

INPUT:

1. Dinosaurs lived long ago (show picture).
 A. Millions of years ago (show number on board and indicate the place value of each digit: 4,000,000).
 B. Before there were humans around (none living today).
 C. Earth looked much different (show picture: moist, big plants, different kinds of animals, and no humans).
2. Dinosaurs became extinct.
 A. Extinct means that there are no more left. All died out.
3. Many dinosaurs were very big.
 A. The size of the bus and bigger (show picture comparing bus to brontosaurus).
4. Dinosaurs were cold-blooded.
 A. Body (blood) was the same temperature as the air around them.
 B. To get warm they would lie in the sun. To get cool the would lie in mud or shade.
5. We are warm-blooded.
 A. Unless we're sick, our bodies are the same temperature all the time (98 degrees).
 B. We sweat to cool off, we wear clothes to warm up (Dinosaurs didn't sweat).
6. Snakes, turtles, and alligators are related to dinosaurs (show picture).
 A. Cold-blooded.
 B. No hair or fur.
7. There were two different kinds of dinosaurs: meat eaters and plant eaters.
8. Meat eaters (show picture of tyrannosaurus rex):
 A. Had long, sharp teeth for tearing meat.
 B. Had strong back legs to move quickly and catch other animals.
 C. Had short front legs with claws used for grabbing.
9. Plant eaters (show picture of brontosaurus):
 A. Had flat teeth for crushing plants (like our back teeth).
 B. Big ones were heavy and slow (like elephant).
 C. Smaller ones were light and fast (like deer or antelope).

ACTIVITY:

1. Classify: Given a number of pictures, students will put animals in groups: meat eaters, plant eaters, or both.
 A. Do several in large group. Include dinosaurs as well as animals living today.
 B. Then, give small groups a series of 15 pictures to classify.

CLOSURE - REVIEW:

1. Small groups will report their results.

Figure 3.3 Criteria for Lesson Plans

Criteria for Lesson Plans

Below are a set of criteria that preservice teachers, teacher educators, and practicing teachers can use with their lesson.

CRITERIA	yes	no	sometimes
1. The lesson is interesting, or informative; values students' ideas; and does not rely on closed-ended questions.			
2. The OBJECTIVE is a short, concise statement that describes exactly what students are to know or be able to do.			
3. All INPUT and ACTIVITY directly support the OBJECTIVE.			
4. The INTRODUCTION is concise and used to introduce students to concepts or material found in the lesson.			
5. The INPUT lists exactly what is taught. A reader would be able to pick up the lesson and teach this lesson. Discussion questions are written out.			
6. Information found in the INPUT is organized and logically sequenced.			
7. If a skill is being taught, guided instruction is used. The independent activity is practice of a skill that has been introduced and practiced in the lesson.			
8. All lesson parts are included and clearly identified: (a) OBJECTIVE, (b) INTRODUCTION, (c) ACTIVITY, and (d) CLOSURE/REVIEW.			
9. The teacher includes reflection as a post-lesson activity.			

ELEMENTS OF EFFECTIVE SKILLS INSTRUCTION

How does one go about teaching thinking skills? Teaching a skill of any kind incorporates four components which are incorporated into this lesson plan form: identification of the procedural components, direct instruction and modeling, guided practice, and independent practice (Collins, Brown, & Neuman, 1989; Hobbs & Schlichter, 1990; Johnson, 1998; Pressley, Harris, & Marks, 1992). Each of these is described below.

1. Identification of the Procedural Components. First, students are introduced to the skill and the specific steps involved are identified. When teaching a thinking skill, this is where students are introduced to the thinking frame used to guide students' thinking during the other steps.

2. Direct Instruction and Modeling. Next, the teacher gives explicit instruction as to how the skill might be used and models it by thinking out loud while going through each step. This element, which is used to provide students with an overview, should be relatively brief.

3. Guided Practice. Guided practice is sometimes referred to as scaffolded instruction (Johnson & Graves, 1997; Rosenshine & Meister, 1992). The goal is to provide the support necessary for students to use the skill independently. Here, the teacher takes the whole class through each step of the skill several times.

4. Independent Practice. Finally, the teacher designs an activity so students can practice the skill independently. This may include homework. If the first three components have been taught effectively, students should be able to complete this activity with 95% -100% success ratio (Brophy, 1986). Independent practice is not meant to be challenging. It is meant to practice those skills already covered in class.

Regular Practice, Review, and Integration

Like any skill, students need to re-visit and review it even after it becomes part of their cognitive repertoire. Regular practice allows for efficiency and automaticity in the use of a thinking skill. Depending on age and ability, learning a new thinking skill might take as few as one lesson or as many as ten lessons for students to be able to use it independently. The skill should be integrated throughout the curriculum. This allows the teacher to provide regular practice, enhance all curriculum areas, raise the level of thinking, augment learning, and create a more interesting and student-centered learning environment.

Lesson Plans for Effective Skills Instruction

The lesson plan form described above is still used with skills instruction. The Objective and Introduction would remain the same. Included under the Input section are (a) identification of the procedural components, and (b) direct instruction and modeling. Included under the Activity section are guided practice and independent practice (see Figure 3.4). Practice, review, and integration happen over time.

Figure 3.4 Sample Thinking Skills Lesson Plan

Teacher: Andrew Johnson   Grade: 5
Subject: Reading   Time: 9:00 - 10:30

OBJECTIVE: Students will learn about the thinking skill, *Creating Groups.*
INTRODUCTION: Boys and girls, today we are going to learn how to use a new thinking skill called Creating Groups.
INPUT:
1. Thinking skills are skills used to help you organize your thoughts.
2. They have specific steps to follow.
3. They make complicated thinking seem easy.
4. Creating Groups is a thinking skill.
 A. Scientists often use this.
 B. Look at animals, organisms, rocks, etc., look for patterns, make sense of things
   by putting them into groups.
5. These are the steps:
 A. Look at the whole.
 B. Identify reoccurring themes or patterns.
 C. Arrange into groups.
 D. Describe.
6. Guided Practice: As a class, brainstorm to list 10 interesting events that have
   happened at school in the last week.
 A. Think out loud (cognitive modeling) to help students organize into groups.
 B. Example: "Are there things that are the same here?"
ACTIVITY:
1. "In your journal, list ten things that have happened so far in the story."
2. Create groups.
3. Describe these events in terms of the groups.
 A. What does this tell you about the story?
 B. Based on the events in your groups, what do you think might happen next?

How Many Skills Do You Teach?

Depending on the level of the students, a teacher might identify four to ten thinking skills to incorporate into his or her classroom each year. It is most effective to focus on one skill at a time while using it in a variety of situations and settings. It is appropriate to spend anywhere from two weeks to a month on a single skill. All thinking skills taught should be reviewed and used throughout the year.

SUMMARY

1. Lesson planning plays an important role in getting student to understand and use thinking skills.
2. Thoughtful lesson planning enhances teacher effectiveness and improves student learning.
3. Lesson plan forms do not need to be complicated to be effective.
4. Most effective lesson plans contain the following components: objective, introduction, input, and activity.
5. To teach a thinking skill, five components are incorporated in this lesson plan form.

References

Clark, C.M., & Dunn, S. (1991). Second-generation research on teachers' planning, intentions, and routines. In H. Waxman & H. Walberg (Eds.), Effective teaching: Current research (pp. 183-201). Berkeley, CA: McCutchan Publishing Corporation.

Clark, C.M., & Peterson, P.L. (1986). Teacher's thought process. In M. Wittrock (Ed.), Handbook of research on teaching (3rd ed.) (pp. 255-296). New York: Macmillan Publishing Company.

Collins, A., Brown, J.S., & Neuman, S. (1989). Cognitive apprenticeship: Teaching the crafts of reading, writing and mathematics. In L.B. Resnick (Ed.), Knowing, learning, and instruction: Essays in honor of Robert Glaser (pp. 453-494). Hillsdale, NJ: Erlbaum.

Freiberg, H.J., & Driscoll, A. (1992). Universal teaching strategies. Needham Heights, MA: Allyn and Bacon.

Hobbs, D.E., & Schlichter, C.L. (1990). Talents Unlimited. In A. Costa (Ed.), Developing minds (Vol. 2). Alexandria, VA: Association of Supervision and Curriculum Development.

Hunter, M. (1984). Knowing, teaching and supervising. In P. Hosford (Ed.), Using what we know about reading. Alexandria, VA: Association for Supervision and Curriculum Development.

Johnson, A. (1998). Word class: A way to modify spelling instruction for gifted learners, The Roeper Review, 20, 128-131.

Johnson, A., & Graves, M. (1997). Scaffolding: A tool for enhancing the reading experience of all students. Texas Journal of Reading, 3, 23-30.

Parker, W.L., & Jarolimek, J. (1997). Social studies in elementary education (10th ed.). Upper Saddle River, NJ: Merrill.

Pressley, M., Harris, K.R., & Marks, M.B. (1992). But good strategy users are constructivists! Educational Psychology Review, 4, 3-31.

Rosenshine, R., & Meister, C. (1992). The use of scaffolds for teaching higher-level cognitive strategies. Educational Leadership, 49, 26-33.

Stringfield, S., & Teddlie, C. (1991). Schools as affecters of teacher effects. In H. Waxman & H. Walberg (Eds.), Effective teaching: Current research (pp. 453-494). Berkeley, CA: McCutchan Publishing Corporation.

Tobin, K., & Fraser, B.M. (1991). Learning from exemplary teachers. In H. Waxman & H. Walberg (Eds.), Effective teaching: Current research (pp. 217-236). Berkeley, CA: McCutchan Publishing Corporation.

Walberg, J.J. (1991). Productive teaching and instruction: Assessing the knowledge base. In H. Waxman & H. Walberg (Eds.), Effective teaching: Current research (pp. 33-62). Berkely, CA: McCutchan Publishing Corporation.

4

Creativity and Creative Thinking Skills

The Chinese tell us that the Tao which can be defined is not the Tao. Perhaps the same might be said of creativity. This chapter examines (a) ideas related to creativity, (b) creativity in the classroom, and (c) creative thinking skills.

WHAT IS CREATIVITY?

Creativity is a cognitive process that leads to new or improved products, performances, or paradigms. It is a quality of thought that allows an individual to generate many ideas, invent new ideas, or recombine existing ideas in a novel fashion (Gallagher & Gallagher, 1994). Rollo May (1975) uses mother-like terms when he describes creativity as a quality in which something new is brought to life. Creativity produces something apart from the ordinary: something remarkable, and something new (Feldman, Csikszentmihalyi, & Gardner, 1994).

There is, however, a difference between being creative and being bizarre. Creativity must have some aesthetic or pragmatic value (Swartz & Perkins, 1990). Unusual is not the same as creative. The arts are littered with short-term wonders who garnered a little bit of attention by being unusual instead of being creative. Once the oddity wears thin, these artists are quickly forgotten without having contributed to their artistic discipline.

Creativity is an action that happens within a domain (Feldman, Csikszentmihalyi, & Gardner, 1994). Mozart displayed his creativity within the domain of music, Freud in psychology, Kurt Vonnegut in literature, Frank Lloyd Wright in architecture, Anthony Hopkins in acting, and Michael Jordan in basketball. All these individuals operated within a particular domain, mastered it, and then pushed it in different directions. Without the domain, their creativity might not exist or be recognized. Mozart, living in a much earlier time or in a different place, probably would not have been able to display his musical talents. Would Michael Jordan be Michael Jordan without basketball?

Creativity and Problem Solving

Creativity involves finding or perceiving problems (Csikszentmihalyi, 1994). Examples: This system needs to be fixed. This idea needs to be expressed. This book needs to be written. This new feeling needs to be incorporated into this dance. Those old theories don't work. Our current scheduling is not getting the job done. There needs to be a book written about thinking skills that teachers can understand and use. This arrangement is boring and mundane. That third movement could be done differently. This way of teaching reading is not working. Creativity also is a matter of problem solving (Gardner, 1993). These problems might be found in all areas including the arts, business, science, the military, or education. Examples: How can the mousetrap be made better? How can this feeling or idea be expressed through movement, dance, music, or visual art? How can this concept be explained? How can this skill be taught? What are we to learn from evil? How can this building be designed most effectively? What kind of a play will allow our team to score a touchdown? Highly creative people are able to solve these kinds of problems by looking at them in different ways (Lipshitze & Waingortin, 1995). That is, they are able to let go of the old ways of thinking, which in turn allows them to generate a variety of novel solutions.

Knowledge, Intelligence, and Creativity

Knowledge is an important component of creativity (Feldhusen, 1995; Gallagher & Gallagher, 1994; Piirto, 1994). Creativity involves the manipulation of ideas from a knowledge base. You cannot have innovative ideas about things you know little about. This is why it is important that teachers design curriculum and units which present students with a fair amount of knowledge that is organized in a way that will help them readily acquire it. Among other things, a well-developed knowledge base enhances students' ability to think creatively and solve problems (Chi, Feltovich, & Glaser, 1981; de Groot, 1965).

There is also some relationship between creativity and intelligence (Good & Brophy, 1990). In their longitudinal study of creativity, Yamada and Tam (1996) found IQ to be one predictor of adult creative behavior and achievement, suggesting that creative productivity requires intelligence. High intelligence is used to facilitate the development of a well-organized knowledge base, thus making it easier to retrieve ideas, relate new information into existing schemas, and to manipulate ideas in new and interesting ways (Feldhusen, 1995). However, while intelligence is required for creative achievement, highly intelligent people are not necessarily highly creative (Starko, 1995).

How Creativity Happens

Creativity seldom happens by accident; rather, it is purposeful, requiring preparation, hard work, and discipline (Marzano et al., 1989). It is not some magical, mystical quality bestowed upon certain humans by the gods. The sudden creative insight that inventors and artists sometimes describe is usually the last step in a long thinking process. Thus, creativity is not an event, but a process. Wallas (1926) proposed four stages of the creative process:

1. Preparation. This is the stage where the problem is first perceived and defined, information about the problem is gathered, and ideas are generated.

2. Incubation. Here, both the conscious and unconscious mind manipulate the problem and think about possible solutions. New information is related to existing information and existing schemata are reorganized to accommodate new information.

3. Illumination. In this stage, the creator suddenly sees the idea, concept, or solution to the problem.

4. Verification. This is an evaluative stage where the creator verifies or tests the idea, concept, or solution.

ENHANCING CREATIVITY IN THE CLASSROOM

Classroom teachers can help to enhance creativity by attending to students' knowledge base, providing a certain amount of freedom to experiment, providing the time to experiment, and by teaching students how to use creative thinking skills.

Knowledge Base

As stated previously, educators need to provide opportunities for children to absorb a great number of concepts if they are to perceive relationships and freely manipulate ideas. There are four ways to enhance this process: First, design well-structured curriculums which are rich in knowledge and experience. In elementary school, science and social studies should be given as much attention as reading and writing, as conceptual knowledge makes reading and writing easier. For middle and high school teachers, knowledge in all subject areas can be enhanced by including literature and a variety of sources along with textbooks and lecture.

Second, relate new information to old. Use familiar things to explain complicated things. Help students find the similarities and see the relationship between ideas by comparing and contrasting, looking for groups or patterns, and by creating metaphors or analogies. This gets students thinking differently about known entities. Examples: How is school like a baseball game? How is writing like creating a watercolor painting? What are the common elements in doing homework, learning how to play a musical instrument, and learning how to serve a volleyball? How is music like writing? How is music like a pencil? How is a pencil like a pig? (They both get smaller with use.)

Third, provide students with a wide variety of experiences. Using literature throughout the curriculum is one way to accomplish this. Here, students are able to have a great many adventures, experience a wide assortment of situations, and accumulate information on a variety of subjects.

And fourth, teachers must attend to their own knowledge base related to learning and to the subjects they are teaching so that they are able to adequately structure learning experiences and guide creative thinkers.

Personal Freedom

In promoting creativity, you can expect a wide range of creative responses, some of which may be silly, obscene, outrageous, or bizarre (Good & Brophy, 1990). Within appropriate limits, students must have the freedom to experiment with ideas and have these types of responses. Appropriate limits, however, will be uniquely defined in each situation. In my college writing courses, students are free to choose their own topics and express their point of view; however, they are asked to consider the amount of personal disclosure appropriate because all assignments are read by other students in this class. I also insist that they be sensitive to the cultural, religious, and political views of other students in this class.

When working with elementary students who are writing or using creative dramatics there is often a tendency to include violence. Having people hit, shot, or killed is often used as a cheap literary device when students don't know what to do with a story. (This happens in the movies all the time.) It is sometimes helpful to tell children that they can be as interesting or creative as they want as long as nobody gets hurt or killed in their stories or dramas. Also, students can be told, in a very unobtrusive manner, if certain words are not suitable for classroom use. Other than this, students should know that their unique ideas are valued and they are free to experiment.

Time

Creativity is enhanced when teachers provide students with the necessary time. Most adults would find it impossible to work in the small segmented blocks of time that we assign students. For example, how many of us could function if we had to think of chemistry for 50 minutes, English for 50 minutes, and literature for another 50 minutes? When time is this frugally parceled out, it would be very hard to experiment with ideas or to creatively apply concepts. There are just too many different ideas to absorb and not enough time to manipulate them. In elementary grades these segmented blocks often become even smaller. (Incidentally, this is why I support a five-year teacher preparation program that many colleges are adopting. It is hard to expect anybody to master the complexities of becoming a good teacher after only two years of general education courses and two years of professional courses.)

So what is the answer? Thematic planning of units which integrate many subject areas along with block scheduling. This will allow for larger more flexible chunks of time and will be more conducive to learning and creativity. Also, it is unreasonable to expect all children to finish their creative products at the same time. Workshop and laboratory approaches to reading, writing, and other subject areas allow students to discover and experiment without having to end at the same time. A rigid curriculum with mandated starting and ending points inhibits creativity.

Teaching Creativity

Various creative processes can be enhanced through instructions (Gallagher & Gallagher, 1995). Navel-Severino (1993) found that children trained in creative thinking scored better on tests of creativity. Piirto (1994) suggests that creative thinking skills transfer to other areas. Teaching creative thinking skills will not only enhance a curriculum, but also increase students' ability to generate ideas and think divergently. To this end, eight creative thinking skills are presented below.

CREATIVE THINKING SKILLS

Creative or divergent thinking has to do with generating ideas, integrating ideas, or seeing things in new ways. Creative thinking complements critical thinking.

1. Fluency: (brainstorming) The student will create the greatest number of ideas without regard to evaluation.
   Thinking Frame
   A. Look at the idea.
   B. Add as many ideas as quickly as you can.

2. Flexibility: The student will create a variety of different approaches.
   Thinking Frame
   A. Look at the original.
   B. Find other ways for it to be used, solved, or applied.

3. Elaboration: The student will embellish an original idea.
   Thinking Frame
   A. Look at the idea.
   B. Add things to it to make it better or more interesting.

4. Originality: The student will produce ideas that are unusual or unique.
   Thinking Frame
   A. Find an idea or problem.
   B. Think of solutions or applications that nobody else has thought of before.

5. Creative Problem Solving (CPS): Given a problem, student will generate solutions.
   Thinking Frame
   A. Look at the problem.
   B. Brainstorm solutions.
   C. Pick one solution.
   D. Elaborate, embellish, and refine.

6. Integrate: The student will connect or combine two or more things to form a new whole.
   Thinking Frame
   A. Look at both things.
   B. Select interesting or important parts.
   C. Combine to describe a new whole.

7. Web and Brainstorm: The student will create a web to generate ideas relative to a given topic.
   Thinking Frame
   A. Look at the original ideas.
   B. Find 2-5 sub-ideas.
   C. Brainstorm on each subheading.
   D. Describe.

8. Generate Relationships: The student will find related items or events.
   Thinking Frame
   A. Look at the item or event.
   B. Generate attributes.
   C. Find items or events with similar or related attributes.
   D. Describe the relationship.

SUMMARY

1. Creativity is a process that leads to a new or improved product, performance, or paradigm.
2. Creative products have aesthetic or pragmatic value.
3. Creativity happens within a domain.
4. Creativity involves finding and solving problems.
5. There is a relationship between creativity, knowledge, and intelligence.
6. Creativity is purposeful.
7. Creative people have an idea to share or a problem to solve.
8. Creativity can be enhanced in the classroom by attending to students' knowledge, freedom, and time and through instruction.

References

Chi, M.T., Feltovish, P.J., & Glaser, R. (1981). Categorization and representation of physics problems by experts and novices. Cognitive Science, 5, 121-152.

DeGroot, A.D. (1965). Thought and choice in chess. The Hague: Mouton.

Elbow, P. (1986). Embracing contraries. New York: Oxford University Press.

Feldhusen, J.F. (1995). Creativity: Knowledge base, metacognitive skills, and personality factors. Journal of Creative Behavior, 29, 255-268.

Feldman, D.H., Csikzentmihalyi, M., & Gardner, H. (1994). Changing the world: A framework for the study of creativity. Westport, CT: Praeger Publishing.

Gallagher, J.J., & Gallagher, S.A. (1994). Teaching the gifted child (4th ed.). Needham Heights, MA: Allyn and Bacon.

Good, T.L., & Brophy, J.E. (1990). Educational psychology: A realistic approach (4th ed.). White Plains, NY: Longman.

Lipshitz, A., & Waingortin, M. (1995). Getting out of ruts: A laboratory study of a cognitive model of reframing. Journal of Creative Behavior, 29, 151-172.

Marzano, R.J., Brandt, R.S., Hughes, C.S., Jones, B.F., Presseisen, B.R., Rankin, S.C., & Suhor, C. (1988). Dimensions of thinking. Alexandria, VA: The Association for Supervision and Curriculum Development.

May, R. (1975). The courage to create. New York: Norton.

Navel-Severino, T. (1993). Cognitive and creative thinking: A comparative study among Filipino children. Gifted Education International, 9, 54-59.

Piirto, J. (1994). Talented children and adults: Their development and education. New York: Macmillan.

Starko, A.J. (1995). Creativity in the classroom. White Plains, NY: Longman.

Swartz, R.J., & Perkins, D.N. (1990). Teaching thinking: Issues and approaches. Pacific Grove, CA: Midwest Publication.

Tishman, S., Perkins, D.N., & Jay, E. (1995). The thinking classroom: Learning and teaching in a culture of thinking. Needham Heights, MA: Allyn and Bacon.

Wallas, G. (1926). The art of thought. New York: Harcourt, Brace, & World.

Yamada, H., & Tam, A.Y. (1996). Prediction study of adult creative achievement: Torrance's longitudinal study of creativity revisited. Journal of Creative Behavior, 30, 144-149.

5

Intelligence and Critical Thinking Skills

I believe that it is the standard definition of intelligence that narrowly constricts our view, treating a certain form of scholastic performance as if it encompasses the range of human capacities and leading to disdain for those who happen not to be psychometrically bright (Gardner, 1996, p. 205).

We know that intelligence is important. Most people would rather have more of it than less of it. But what is it? Is it the ability to produce high scores on certain tests? Is it the ability to remember information? Is it the ability to process numbers quickly? Or is it the ability to learn musical instruments, languages, sports, or computer programs? This chapter will examine (a) a traditional view of intelligence, (b) multiple intelligences, and (c) critical thinking skills.

A TRADITIONAL VIEW OF INTELLIGENCE

Traditionally it was believed that intelligence was something that could be measured and neatly described with a number. Students took a test, the number of errors were subtracted from the total number possible, and a score was given. This score was compared to the scores of large groups of students of the same age. Students were then ranked according to where their scores fell within this same-age group. They were given a percentile ranking which showed how many same-age students scored above and below them. Finally, numbers were assigned to each percentile rank and this number was said to indicate intelligence (Walters & Gardner, 1985). Those who had bigger numbers had more of it, and those with smaller numbers had less of it. This number came to be called intelligence quotient or IQ. The problem with this view, however, is that it is offers a very narrow definition of what intelligence is (Armstrong, 1994; Gardner, 1994).

Existing in Multiple Words

While the types of norm-reference intelligence tests described above are fairly accurate predictors of a student's ability to do well in a school environment, it remains that most students do eventually leave school. The problems encountered in these new non-school worlds are different than those encountered in school worlds. Suddenly, nobody is asking them to read a paragraph and choose the best of four responses. Nobody wants to know what time west-bound trains might meet east-bound trains. And nobody cares what the climax and resolution of a story might be. Instead, there are others types of problems to be solved: children to be raised, cars to fix, computer programs to use, speeches to write, businesses to run, budgets to plan, jobs to land, deals to make, people to educate, committees with which to deal, houses to build, candidates to elect, and community issues to resolve; all of which have nothing to do with east-bound and west-bound trains.

All people eventually discover that they are pretty smart in some areas and not very smart in others and that a number ascribed to them on some test during their school years does not adequately predict or describe their ability to solve the kinds of problems existing in non-school worlds. Does that mean norm-referenced ability tests are useless? No. It simply means that they are limited in what they measure and predict and should always be used in conjunction with many other types of measures when describing students' ability or potential to perform.

MULTIPLE INTELLIGENCES

Intelligence is not a one-dimensional entity falling on a straight-line continuum. "There is no correspondence between an IQ score and the size or functioning efficiency of the brain or any particular part of it, and there is no single ability that we can call intelligence" (Good & Brophy, 1995, p. 516). People are not more intelligent or less intelligent as much as they are intelligent in different ways. For example, the type of intelligence displayed by an indigenous person living in the jungles of South America is much different than that of a stockbroker working on Wall Street in New York. The type of intelligence displayed by Michael Jordan on a basketball court is different than that of Kurt Vonnegut writing books, Robin Williams creating comedy, or B.B. King playing a blues solo on his guitar. Each domain utilizes a different type of intelligence to achieve mastery. Different environments value domains differently.

Howard Gardner's book <u>Frames of Mind</u> (1983) was instrumental in getting school worlds to start thinking about intelligence in much broader terms. He defined intelligence as the ability to solve problems or create products which are valued within a culture setting. Instead of a single entity with many facets,

Gardner has identified eight intelligences (Checkley, 1997), all of which work together as a system:

1. Linguistic intelligence is the ability to use words to describe or communicate ideas. Examples -- poet, writer, storyteller, comedian, public speaker, public relations, politician, journalist, editor, or professor.

2. Logical-mathematical intelligence is the ability to perceive patterns in numbers or reasoning, to use numbers effectively, or to reason well. Examples -- mathematician, scientist, computer programmer, statistician, logician, or detective.

3. Spatial intelligence is the ability to perceive the visual-spatial world accurately (not get lost) and to transform it. Examples -- hunter, scout, guide, interior decorator, architect, artist, or sculptor.

4. Bodily-kinesthetic intelligence is expertise in using one's body. Examples -- actor, athlete, mime, or dancer.

5. Musical intelligence is the ability to recognize and produce rhythm, pitch, and timber; to express musical forms; and to use music to express an idea. Examples -- composer, director, performer, or musical technician.

6. Interpersonal intelligence is the ability to perceive and appropriately respond to the moods, temperaments, motivations, and needs of other people. Examples -- pastor, counselor, administrator, teacher, manager, coach, co-worker, or parent.

7. Intrapersonal intelligence is the ability to access one's inner life, to discriminate one's emotions, intuitions, and perceptions, and to know one's strengths and limitations. Examples -- religious leader, counselor, psychotherapist, writer, or philosopher.

8. Naturalistic intelligence is the ability to recognize and classify living things (plants, animals) as well as sensitivity to other features of the natural world (rocks, clouds). Examples -- naturalist, hunter, scout, farmer, or environmentalist.

Intelligences Are Independent

Each one of these seven intelligences operates independently of the other: meaning that if one is strong in music it does not necessarily mean one will be strong in mathematics. A person can have outstanding ability in one area and yet be very limited in another. For example, Gardner describes Sigmund Freud as having outstanding linguistic, interpersonal, and intrapersonal intelligence, while being weak in the areas of natural sciences, mathematics, or anything quantitative (Gardner, 1995). Of Albert Einstein, he writes, "Einstein felt that he did not have great mathematical gifts and deliberately chose not to take courses and to continue in that area" (p. 103). Each intelligence is independent of the other, yet all of them, working together, are used to solve problems and fashion products.

Classroom Implications

The following are suggestions for applying the idea of multiple intelligence to a classroom:

1. Provide elementary students with a wide variety of experiences in order to help them discover their interests and talents. In the adolescent years, help students to find and develop those intelligences which may lead to future vocational or avocational pursuits (Walter & Gardner, 1985).

2. Use multiple criteria to describe students as learners. Instead of using only standardized test scores, use learning portfolios to show students' growth over time. These portfolios should contain a meaningful collection of students' work that illustrates various types of thinking and problem solving.

3. Encourage students to complete assignments or projects in ways other than writing reports or answering homework questions. Figure 5.1 shows alternative methods for demonstrating knowledge.

Figure 5.1 Alternative Ways to Demonstrate Knowledge

Alternative Ways to Demonstrate Knowledge

- create a poem
- put important items on a
  time line
- create a semantic web
- put events or ideas in
  categories
 - create and give a speech
- weigh or measure
- plan and perform a
  newscast
- design a crossword
  puzzle
	- make a game or design a
	  quiz show
	- create a sculpture or
	  painting
	- create a radio drama
	- create a bulletin board
	- design a poster
	- design a survey
	- tape an interview
	- create a play
	- run an experiment
		- make a commercial
		- use dance or mime to
		  express an idea
		- create a rap song
		- design a reading guide
		- find related issues
		- describe an idea using
		  numbers
		- describe multiple
		  viewpoints
		- write a newspaper article

4. Plan assignments and activities which use each type of intelligence. For example, while studying a unit on American states, have students write an ad or commercial to attract tourists (linguistic); determine how many people there are per square mile and compare it to their own state (mathematical); draw a picture that will be used as a poster to promote tourism (spatial); play charades to answer questions based on important items related to that state (bodily-kinesthetic); find or write songs that could be used as background music in a radio commercial promoting tourism (musical); work in cooperative groups to identify ten important historical events and arrange them on a time line (interpersonal); identify four reasons why they might enjoy living in that state and four things that they would miss if they moved (intrapersonal); and use an observational notebook to record and describe changes in a local environment (naturalist).

5. Use the smart chart to find examples of people, characters, or events in the newspaper, literature, community, or school that demonstrate the different types of intelligence (Figure 5.2).

Figure 5.2 Smart Chart

Smart Chart

Find an example of characters or events in the newspaper, literature, or community where the following kinds of intelligences are displayed:

Word Smart:

Logic or Math Smart:

Space Smart:

Body Smart:

Music Smart:

People Smart:

Feelings Smart:

Nature Smart:

Other Kinds of Smart:

Interpersonal and Intrapersonal Intelligence

Teachers often have difficulty designing activities which incorporate interpersonal and intrapersonal intelligence. Thus, this section describes two strategies which can be used to this end: cooperative learning and a feelings chart.

Cooperative Learning

Cooperative learning is an effective learning tool which utilizes interpersonal intelligence (Johnson & Johnson, 1984). It is not the same as having students work in groups. Cooperative learning is a structured learning activity consisting of five elements:

1. Positive interdependence. Students perceive they are linked with group members so they cannot succeed unless everyone does his or her part. They sink or swim together. This element is best achieved by designing activities that have specific roles. Various roles are listed in Figure 5.3.

Figure 5.3 Roles for Cooperative Learning Activities

Roles for Cooperative Learning Groups

1. President: Makes final decisions. Appoints other roles.
2. Reader: Reads the material out loud.
3. Recorder/Scribe: Records ideas.
4. Sociologist: Checks to see how the group is doing on social skills (use matrix).
5. Checker: Checks to make sure everyone's voice or ideas are heard. Makes sure each person has contributed an idea.
6. Encourager: Looks for good ideas to note and encourages full
7. Speaker/Explainer: Describes the group's decision, explains.
8. Summarizer: Restates the group's major conclusions or answer.
9. Artist: Creates a visual image to correspond with knowing.
10. Dancer/Mime: Creates or performs movement to correspond with assignment.
11. Musician: Sings - performs - or describes songs and lyrics that correspond with assignment.
12. Materials Handler: Gets necessary materials to finish the task.
13. Checker: Checks on the learning by asking group members to explain, summarize material.
14. Time Keeper: Keeps track of time.
15. Energizer: Energizes the group when it start to lag.
16. Researcher: Gets needed information or material.
17. Brain: Helps think of answers/ideas.

---

2. Individual accountability. There are no hitchhikers. The performance of each individual is assessed and the results are given back to the group. Individual accountability can be achieved in a number of ways: (a) one person is picked at random to explain the group's ideas; (b) students do assignments together; however, one group member's assignment is picked at random and that score given to all; (c) all students sign off on the project; (d) students receive the average of their group totals for a graded assignment; or (e) each person describes his or her role in the project on a separate sheet of paper.

3. Group processing. In a large group or small groups, time is taken at the end of the activity to process how well the group did in accomplishing the task and working effectively in a group.

4. Social skills. Students are taught the social (interpersonal) skills necessary to function in a group (Figure 5.4). Before the cooperative learning activity, the teacher should introduce a new social skill and models it. During the activity, anecdotal records or checklists are used to look for that skill (Figure 5.5).

Figure 5.4 Social Skills for Cooperative Learning

Social Skills Used for Cooperative Learning

Forming Skills
1. Move into groups quietly.
2. Stay with the group.
3. Use quiet voices.
4. Take turns.
5. Keep hands and feet to yourself.

Functioning Skills
1. All group member need to share ideas.
2. Look at the speaker.
3. Use each other's names.
4. Express support and acceptance.
5. Ask for help or clarification when needed.
6. Energize the group when necessary.

Discussion Skills
1. Summarize or restate.
2. Describe feelings.
3. Criticize ideas, not people.
4. Ask for justification: Ask members to give facts and reasons.

---

5. *Structuring a cooperative learning activity.* The following tips are helpful in designing a cooperative learning activity: (a) have a specific task in mind, (b) describe the criteria for successful completion of the task, (c) assign roles, (d) monitor group progress, and (e) take time at the end to process the experience. Figure 5.6 shows a sample lesson plan in which a cooperative learning activity is used.

Figure 5.5 Checklist for Social Skills

Skills for Cooperative Learning

	Group1	Group2	Group 3	Group 4
I. FORMING SKILLS				
1. Move quickly and quietly into groups.				
2. Stay with the group.				
3. Use quiet voices.				
4. Take turns.				
II. FUNCTIONING SKILLS				
1. Share ideas and opinions.				
2. Look at the speaker.				
3. Use each other's names.				
4. Express support and acceptance.				
III. DISCUSSION SKILLS				
1. Summarize or restate.				
2. Describe feelings.				
3. Criticize ideas, not people.				
4. Ask for justification.				

Figure 5.6 Lesson Plan Using a Cooperative Learning Activity

Grade 5

OBJECTIVE: Students will learn about interpersonal intelligence.
INTRODUCTION: This week, we've learned about several different ways to be smart. Today we're going to learn about a new intelligence called interpersonal intelligence.
INPUT:
1. There are many ways to be smart.
2. Interpersonal intelligence is another way to be smart.
3. (Write "interpersonal" on the board.) Is there a part of this word that you recognize? What might give us a clue as to what it might mean?
 A. Help students to see "inter" and "personal."
 B. Inter means between. Personal refers to a person.
4. This means you are very good at work between people or with people.
 A. You know how to organize them.
 B. You are aware of their feelings.
5. Examples: coaches, teachers, and managers all need to be able to organize and
   work with people.
ACTIVITY:
1. Students are put in cooperative groups of four.
2. Roles: (a) president, makes all decisions, appoints others and keeps track of time; (b) scribe, records ideas; (c) speaker, shares group's ideas with large group, (d) artist, creates a visual aid to help illustrate an important idea.
3. Task: Look through the newspaper to find at least five examples of
   interpersonal intelligence (allow 20 minutes).
 A. Examples of people who have had to be people smart in order to accomplish
   something.
 B. Examples of people who are very good at working with other people.
4. Scribe: Record the name of the person and what that person did.
5. Artist: Create a picture, chart, or some visual aid that helps explain what the   group found.
6. Speaker: Share group's ideas with the class.
7. Students will complete the task and share. The teacher will recognize
   outstanding creativity and groups that worked well together.

Feelings Chart

Intrapersonal intelligence is used to help students explore their interior worlds, and to discover and use their intuitions, feelings, and imagination. A feelings chart can be used here. This technique helps students analyze different characters' reactions to similar events. Eventually these ideas are applied to their own lives.

After reading a story, the teacher begins the activity by identifying three or four story events. Using the feelings chart (Figure 5.7), these events are listed vertically in the column marked "events." Two to four story characters are then listed horizontally along the top of the chart. Students describe each character's reaction to each of the events. This activity can also be applied to social studies by using real life events found in history or the news.

Figure 5.7 Feelings Chart

Feelings Chart

Characters

Events	

To extend this, the feelings comparison chart is used (Figure 5.8). Here, students use the event or feeling from the story to identify similar events and feelings from their own lives. These ideas are shared in small groups.

Figure 5.8 Feelings Comparison Chart

Feelings Comparison Chart

Find an event from the story. Pick one character from the story. Describe that person's feelings related to the event. Then describe an event from your own life that caused similar feelings.

Story Event	Character's Feelings	Your Life Event/Feelings

CRITICAL THINKING SKILLS

Critical or convergent thinking has to do with organizing, analyzing, evaluating, or describing what is already there. This type of thinking generally leads the thinker towards a specific conclusion. Critical thinking complements creative thinking. Eleven critical thinking skills are described here.

1. Inferring: The student will go beyond the available information to identify what may reasonably be true.
   Thinking Frame
   A. Identify what is known.
   B. Identify similar situations.
   C. Make a reasonable guess based on A and B.

2. Compare: Given two or more items, students will find their similarities.
   Thinking Frame
   A. Look at all items.
   B. Brainstorm attributes of each.
   C. Conclude and describe.

3. Compare and Contrast: Given two or more items, the student will find their similarities and differences.
   Thinking Frame
   A. Look at all items.
   B. Find the similarities.
   C. Find the differences.
   D. Conclude and describe.

4. Analyze: Students will break an item or event down into its component parts.
   Thinking Frame
   A. Look at the item or event.
   B. Find important parts.
   C. Describe each part.

5. Supporting a Statement: Students will use appropriate reasons, detail, or examples to support a statement or conclusion.
   Thinking Frame
   A. Make a statement or claim.
   B. Gather information to support the statement.
   C. Organize the information.
   D. Describe the original statement in terms of the new information.

6. Decision Making: Students will examine the options and alternatives in order to decide on a course of action.
   Thinking Frame
   A. Identify the problem or decision.
   B. Generate options.
   C. Evaluate costs and rewards of options.
   D. Make a choice based on the above.

7. Ordering: Given a criterion, students will arrange events, concepts, or items in sequential order based on that criterion.
   Thinking Frame
   A. Look at or define a criterion.
   B. Look at the whole.
   C. Arrange items within the whole according to the criterion.
   D. Describe the whole in terms of the new order.

8. Evaluation/Critique: The student will make a formal evaluation based on a set of criteria.
   Thinking Frame
   A. Look at or define a criterion.
   B. Look at the subject.
   C. Compare the subject to the criterion.
   D. Describe the subject relative to the criterion.

9. Creating Groups: Students will impose order on a field by identifying and grouping common themes or patterns.
   Thinking Frame
   A. Look at the whole.
   B. Identify reoccurring items, themes, or patterns.
   C. Arrange into groups.
   D. Describe the whole in terms of groups.

10. Investigation: The student will find information to answer a question.
    Thinking Frame
    A. Ask question.
    B. Collect data.
    C. Organize data.
    D. Answer question.

11. Experimenting: The student will experiment to answer a question.
    Thinking Frame
    A. Ask a question.
    B. Experiment and collect data.
    C. Organize data.
    D. Answer question.

SUMMARY

1. Traditional views offer a very narrow view of intelligence.
2. Scores on intelligence tests have limited predictive value outside a school environment.
3. The theory of multiple intelligences takes a much broader view of intelligence.
4. The theory of multiple intelligences describes eight intelligences which work together to solve problems and fashion products: linguistic intelligence, logical-mathematical intelligence, spatial intelligence, bodily-kinesthetic intelligence, musical intelligence, interpersonal intelligence, intrapersonal

intelligence, and naturalist intelligence.
5. Each intelligence operates independently of the other.
6. Cooperative learning can be used to facilitate interpersonal intelligence.
7. A feelings chart can be used to facilitate intrapersonal intelligence.

References

Armstrong, T. (1994). Multiple intelligence in the classroom. Alexandria, VA: Association for Supervision and Curriculum Development.

Checkley, K. (1997). The first seven ... and the eighth: A conversation with Howard Gardner. Educational Leadership, 55, 8-13.

Gardner, H. (1983). Frames of mind. New York: HarperCollins.

Gardener, H. (1986). The waning of intelligence tests. In R. Sternberg & D. Detterman (Eds.), What is intelligence? Norwood, NJ: Ablex Publishing Corporation.

Gardner, H. (1996). Reflection on multiple intelligence: Myths and messages. Phi Delta Kappan, 77, 200-209.

Good, T., & Brophy, J. (1995). Contemporary educational psychology (5th ed.). White Plains, NY: Longmann.

Sternberg, R. (1990). Metaphors of mind: Conceptions of the nature of intelligence. New York: Press Syndicate of the University of Cambridge.

Walters, J.M., & Gardener, H. (1985). The development and education of intelligences, in F. Link (Ed.), Essays on the intellect. Alexandria, VA: Association for Supervision and Curriculum Development.

6

Thinking Skills and Reading

This chapter describes four areas related to thinking skills and reading instruction: (a) reading and the reading process, (b) thinking skill activities for narrative texts, (c) thinking skill activities for expository text, and (d) thinking skills and comprehension.

READING

Reading is much more than learning a series of phonetic skills so that words can be sounded out. Rather, reading is learning how to use print to create meaning. To do this, readers use the information in their head to make sense of the information found on the page. Reading then is an interaction between the text and readers' knowledge and experiences.

Reading is also a constantly developing skill. This means that just like learning a musical instrument, we get better by practicing. And likewise, if we do not practice, we do not improve. Part of our jobs as teachers is to design interesting activities that will motivate students to practice reading and to keep them engaged with the text. Thinking skills can be used to this end.

A distinction must be made here between narrative and expository texts. The purpose for reading a narrative text is to enjoy the story. The goal for the teacher here is to get students to enter into the story, to relive it in some way, or to create associations to real life emotions or experiences. This is called an aesthetic response to literature (Rosenblatt, 1983; Zarillo, 1991). Activities and questions for narrative text are be designed to engage the reader's emotions and imagination.

Expository texts, on the other hand, have the sole purpose of informing students. The goal here is to extract information, organize and examine information, and construct meaning. Activities and questions for expository text should be designed to help students manipulate or use the information found in the text.

THINKING SKILLS AND NARRATIVE TEXT

In order to make reading accessible to readers of all levels, scaffolded reading experiences are used (Graves, Juel, & Graves, 1998; Johnson & Graves, 1997). These consist of three parts: pre-reading, during-reading, and post-reading activities. The pre-reading activity is used to activate relevant schema prior to reading and to give students a preview or overview of the upcoming text. For during-reading activities, students most often read silently or with a partner. For low-ability readers, outlines, advanced organizers, and audiotapes are used here to help them read independently. Post-reading activities get students to manipulate ideas or emotions experienced during the reading of the story.

Pre-Reading Activities

The book <u>Wrinkle in Time</u> by Madeleine L'Engle (1962) is used to illustrate how these thinking skills might be applied to narrative text. Teachers are encouraged to adapt or modify each thinking skill to suit their teaching situation.

1. Fluency. Students brainstorm on related topics prior to reading to activate relevant schemata. Their ideas are listed on the front board. To extend this, the teacher next asks students to create groups (*Creating Groups*) out of the list or put the items in some sort of sequential order (*Ordering*). Example: Before reading <u>Wrinkle in Time</u> with a sixth grade class, the teacher tells students that they are about to read a story in which the main characters battle evil. Students are then asked to brainstorm to generate a list of evil characters. Students then examine their list and organize the characters into groups (TV characters, historical characters, real life characters, etc.). This list can also be put in some sort of sequential order such as most interesting to least interesting, most evil to least evil, most dangerous to least dangerous, most recent to least recent, or closest to farthest away.

2. Creative Problem Solving. Students are presented with a problem found in a chapter or story. They brainstorm to find the best solution, refine their idea, then share their idea with the class (Figure 6.1). As described in Chapter 3, this thinking skill activity should be done in large group first, but eventually move to small groups, pairs, and individuals. Students' solutions can be recorded in reading logs. *Creative Problem Solving* will lead to a wide variety of solutions. Unique, creative, or very practical responses can be recognized and displayed on a bulletin board along with diagrams or necessary explanations.

Example: In Chapter 1 of <u>Wrinkle in Time</u>, a strange little woman knocks on the door in the middle of a dark, stormy night. She is soaked to the bone. Her boots are wet and she can't take them off by herself. How might this problem be solved?

Figure 6.1 CPS

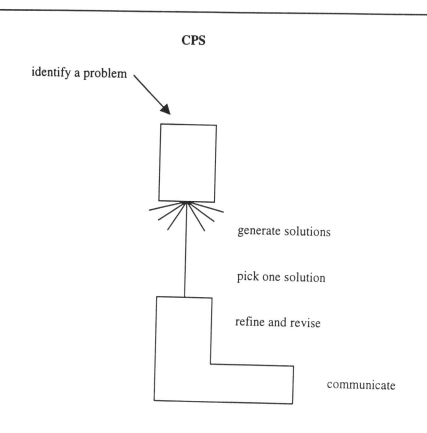

CPS

identify a problem

generate solutions

pick one solution

refine and revise

communicate

3. Web and Brainstorm. This thinking skill is also used to activate relevant schemata. Here the teacher announces a theme or topic found in the upcoming story selection. This is put in a circle on the front board. Students are asked to think of three items or subtopics related to the original theme. Nodes are created for the subtopics. Students then brainstorm on each node. After reading, students add to the original web. This technique is much better than comprehension worksheets in helping the teacher to assess how students are processing the story. An example of this thinking skill used for Wrinkle in Time is shown in Figure 6.2.   Here the theme is evil and the three subtopics or associations are darkness, creatures, and destruction.

Figure 6.2 Web and Brainstorm

Web and Brainstorm

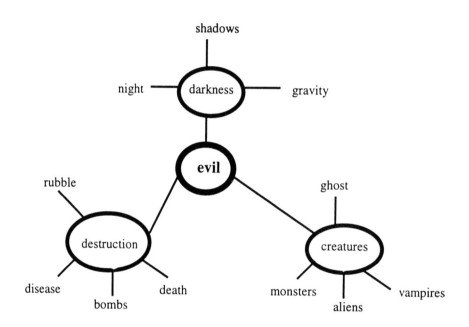

---

4. *Compare. Comparing* is used to find the similarity between two or more items or events found in the upcoming reading selection. These should be items with which students are already familiar. When looking at two items, a T-chart is used to list their attributes and find their similarities. Example: In Chapter 2 of <u>Wrinkle in Time</u>, Meg has a very bad day at school. Have students compare their very bad days with one of their classmates. Here they use a T-chart to

brainstorm attributes of each, then look for common themes in order to reach a conclusion (Figure 6.3). To make multiple comparisons, a Compare-O-Graph is used (Figure 6.4).

Figure 6.3 Comparing T-Chart

T-Chart

my bad day at school	Jackie's bad day at school
got up late	stubbed my toe
soggy breakfast	no toothpaste
no seat on the bus	missed the bus
didn't finish homework	dropped the ball in gym class
got teased	ripped my pants
got yelled at	didn't understand math

Conclusions:

---

5. Compare and Contrast. This thinking skill is used to compare and contrast familiar items or events found in the upcoming text. Example: Before reading Chapter 9 in Wrinkle in Time, students use the Web-of-Comparison to compare and contrast good and evil characters (Figure 6.5). These characters can be taken from a book, movie, history, or recent events. Other examples: Students can compare and contrast two heroes, two evil characters, two books written by the same author, or two books written by different authors.

6. Creating Groups and *Fluency.* Examples of these are shown under *Fluency* above.

Figure 6.4 Compare-O-Graph

Compare-O-Graph

	Me	Jackie	Meg	Billy
bad days at school				

Figure 6.5 Web-of-Comparison

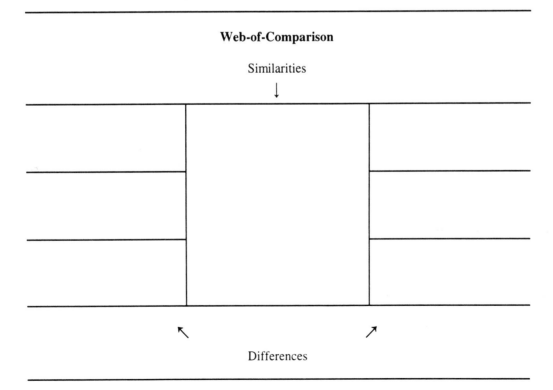

Web-of-Comparison

Similarities

↓

Differences

Post-Reading Activities

Here the teacher designs activities which allow students to interact with the ideas or events found in the text. For narrative text, avoid activities which simply ask students to recount story details. Keep in mind that the purpose of reading narrative text is always to enjoy the story.

1. Fluency. Students brainstorm to create a list of things related to the story: (a) interesting or important events; (b) associations related to a scene, character, or event; (c) particular items that might be found in a particular scene; or (d) alternative responses to a particular problem or situation. Like before, these are recorded and used to create groups or put in some sort of sequential order.

2. Elaboration. Students examine characters, events, scenes, or items in a story and (a) add interesting details; (b) describe other items which might be included; (c) add details or descriptive adjectives to sentences; (d) add other interesting characters, events, or items not included; or (e) create a drawing of a scene or event adding details the author did not describe. Example: Chapter 1 includes a scene in Meg's bedroom up in the attic. Say to students, "You are up in this attic. Look all around you and describe what you see." Or, "Add more details to the description of one of the characters to make that character more interesting."

3. Creative Problem Solving. Here students find a problem in the story and brainstorm to create alternative solutions (Figure 6.1).

4. Integrate. In their reading logs, as part of a creative writing assignment or when doing creative dramatics, students add characters or events from another story. Example: "What would happen in Chapter 6 of Wrinkle in Time if Glinda the Good Witch from The Wizard of Oz suddenly appeared?"

5. Web and Brainstorm. Students add details to the pre-reading web or create new webs to describe the chapter or story. This is also an example of the thinking skill *Analyze,* as students must break the whole into its component parts and describe it.

6. Generate Relationships. Students describe events or feelings that are similar to those found in the story or chapter. Examples: "In Chapter 12, Meg had to face danger and was afraid. Describe (a) a time when you were afraid, (b) a time when you had to do something you didn't want to, (c) other heros or lead characters who have faced anger, (d) people or other characters that remind you of a character from the story, or (e) events that remind you of those found in the story."

7. Infer. Students use information found in the story along with their own knowledge to make guesses or assumptions about things not described. An Infer-O-Gram can be used here (see Figure 6.6). Examples: "What might have happened in Chapter 12 if Meg had failed?" Or, "Describe Meg and Calvin's friendship at school in the upcoming year." Students might also use inference to make a guess as to what might happen next in the story.

Figure 6.6 Infer-O-Gram

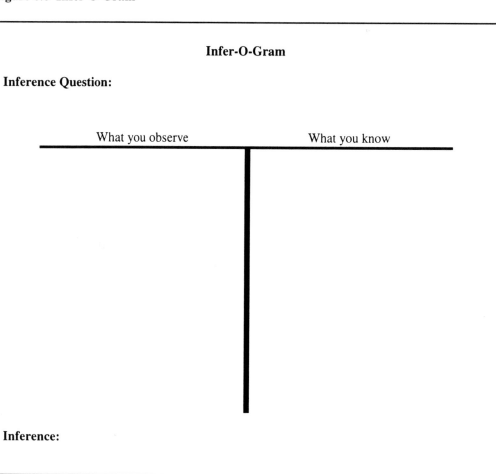

Infer-O-Gram

Inference Question:

What you observe   What you know

Inference:

8. Compare. This thinking skill is used to find the similarity between two or more items found in the story or elsewhere. Examples: Students compare (a) Meg and Dorothy from the <u>Wizard of Oz</u>, (b) this book to other books, (c) this chapter to previous chapters, (d) events here to events in real life, (e) characters here to characters found in real life, or (f) a descriptive paragraph here to another writer's or student's descriptive paragraphs. For an interesting inquiry assignment, have students pick out a 100-word section from the story. Count the number of adjectives found there. Then, compare to a 100-word segment from other books. The results can be displayed using a line graph. What conclusions, if any, can students make regarding authors and adjectives? (Inquiry will be described in further detail in Chapter 8.)

9. Compare and Contrast. Students compare and contrast two items or events found in the story, or compare and contrast a story event to another event. Examples: Students compare and contrast (a) the beginning of the book to the end, b) Meg in Chapter 1 to Meg in Chapter 6, (c) Meg to another story character, (d) Meg to someone the students knows, (e) a character in the story to the student, (f) an event in the story to an event in students' lives, or (g) this story to another story.

10. Analyze. This thinking skill is used to break the story into its component parts and describe it. For example: In Wrinkle in Time, students might describe (a) important story events found in the beginning, middle, and end of the story; (b) the good, bad, and inauspicious story events; or (c) real things, possible things, and imaginary things found in the story. The teacher can also ask students to decide how the story might best be broken into parts and how each part might be best described.

11. Supporting a Statement. Students make a statement, then use clues or sentences found in the story to support it. Examples: In Wrinkle in Time, students look for clues to support one of the following the statements: (a) Meg is a hero, (b) Meg likes Calvin, (c) Charles Wallace might become a scientist, (d) Charles Wallace has ESP, or (e) Mrs. Whatsit is a magical character (see Figure 6.7).

Figure 6.7 Support a Statement

Support a Statement

Statement	Supporting Clues or Information

12. Evaluation/Critique. Students first generate criteria for a good book, then use these criteria to rate the book. Their ratings can also be used to make comparisons with other books (see Figure 6.8).

Figure 6.8 Evaluation/Critique

Rating Books

Book -- Wrinkle in Time

Criteria	*Rating*
interesting characters	4
good story	3
action or adventure	4
hero or strong lead character	3

Total: 14

Rating: 4 = very high, 3 = good, 2 = average, 1 = low

Ranking Books

	Criteria				
Book:	1	2	3	4	**Total**
Wrinkle in Time	4	3	3	2	12
Bridge to Teribithia	3	1	1	1	6
The Hatchet	1	4	4	4	13
Where the Red Fern Grows	2	2	2	3	9

Ranking: 4 = highest; 1 = lowest

Criterion
1. interesting characters
2. good story
3. action or adventure
4. hero or strong lead character

---

13. Investigation. Students gather and organize data found in the story in order to make a conclusion or answer a question. For example, in Chapter 12 of <u>Wrinkle in Time</u>, how many and what kinds of adjectives are found? Students list the adjectives, put them in groups, and use tally marks to indicate the number in each group. These data are put on a graph and comparisons are made to other chapters or stories. Students might also examine the numbers and types of many kinds of things including nouns, characters, events, brave things, foolish things, big things, little things, important things, magical things, or normal things.

Using Thinking Skills to Respond to Narrative Text

The following questions, based on thinking skills, will elicit an aesthetic response and can be used as writing or discussion prompts:
1. Record a passage or part of the story that you find interesting. Tell why you recorded it.
2. Describe a time when you had a similar situation or feeling as one described in the story.
3. Which character is your favorite? Why?
4. Which character is your least favorite? Why?
5. How are you like one of the characters?
6. Create a Web-of-Comparison using you and a character from the story.
7. Create a Web-of-Comparison using a book character and a real life character.
8. What things in this story remind you of your life?
9. If you were a teacher, would you read this book to your class? Why?
10. What were the five most interesting things that happened in this story? Put them in order from happiest to saddest.
11. Ask a question of one of the characters in this story and write what you think the character's answer might be.
12. Describe a problem a character in your book faces and predict how you think that character will solve it.
13. Where and when did this story take place? Find clues to support your guess.
14. If you appeared someplace in this story, what might you see? What might you do?
15. Describe a thought or feeling that went through your head as you read.
16. What other books or movies does this story remind you of?
17. Describe something interesting or important in the story that other people might not have noticed.
18. Draw a picture, create a diagram, or design a symbol that might represent an interesting or important part of this story.

19. How does the author make this book interesting?
20. How would you change this book if you were the author?
21. Does the title fit? What other titles might be used instead?
22. Describe something that might happen after the story has ended. Find at least three clues to support your idea.
23. Would you recommend this book to others? What kind of person might enjoy this story?
24. Write a letter to somebody you think might like this book. Convince that person to read it.
25. Record a short dialogue in which you talk to somebody in this book.
26. Write a newspaper headline and an article for an event in this book.
27. How does the author portray female characters? How are their roles like male characters?
28. Write a journal entry for one of the characters found in this book.
29. Break the story or chapter into beginning, middle, and ending parts. List the three most important events in each part.

THINKING SKILLS AND EXPOSITORY TEXT

The purpose for reading expository text is to extract information. Scaffolded reading, as described previously, and reading logs can also be used here.

Pre-Reading Activities

1. Fluency. Students generate ideas about a topic before reading to activate relevant schemata.

2. Web and Brainstorm. Students web and brainstorm before reading to create a semantic map to activate and organize relevant schemata.

* More pre-reading activities are described below in the section on comprehension skills.

Post-Reading Activities

1. Generate Relationships. Students find similar items, ideas, or events as those described in the text.

2. Compare. Students compare items, ideas, or events found in the text to those found elsewhere.

3. Compare and Contrast. Students compare and contrast items, ideas, or events found in the text to those found elsewhere.

4. Creating Groups. Students generate a list of interesting or important items, ideas, or events found in the text, then look for themes or reoccurring patterns to create groups. Finally, the text is described in terms of those groups.

5. Support a Statement. A statement is made relative to an item, idea, or event found in the text (Figure 6.7). Students then gather clues found in the text to support it.

6. Order. Students generate and record a list of interesting or important ideas or items found in the text. These are then put in order relative to a given criterion. Examples: (a) most important to least important, (b) familiar to strange, (c) easy to difficult, (d) soft to hard, (e) most likely to float to least likely to float, or (f) big to little.

7. Evaluation/Critique. Students generate three to five criteria for a well-written chapter or book. The current text is then rated from 1- 4 on those criteria. This evaluation can be used to compare the current text or chapter to others (see Figure 6.8).

THINKING SKILLS AND COMPREHENSION

A comprehension skill is a type of thinking skill. Just like a thinking skill, it is a cognitive process that can be broken down into parts and taught using explicit instruction. Teachers can help students learn to comprehend expository text by approaching comprehension skills in the same way as thinking skills. Comprehension skills should be used only with expository text.

Comprehension

Comprehension is the act of constructing meaning with a text (Dole, Duffy, Roehler, & Pearson, 1991). Here, the reader plays an active role, using information in his or her head to filter, organize, interpret, and generate relationships with the incoming information and to ultimately construct meaning (Fielding & Pearson, 1994; Fitzpatrick, 1994; Gunning, 1996; Reutzel & Cooter, 1996). Comprehension is an interaction between word identification, knowledge, and comprehension skills (Cunningham, Moore, Cunningham, & Moore, 1995).

The Need for Comprehension Skills

Currently, little time is spent in most classrooms teaching children how to comprehend text (Reutzel & Cooter, 1996). Instead, much of reading instruction is spent developing accurate and automatic word identification skills and increasing oral reading fluency; however, these do not guarantee that students will develop the skills needed to comprehend expository text (Cunningham & Wall, 1994). And, while wide reading is important, this also does little to prepare students for careful, thoughtful reading of expository texts. Finally, simply exposing students to comprehension worksheets or other tasks requiring them to recall information found in a text also does very little to increase their comprehension skills (Dole et al., 1991; Reutzel & Cooter, 1996). What is needed is explicit instruction in the use of comprehension skills to help students increase their ability to comprehend texts independently (Guthere, Van Meter, McCann, Wigfield, Bennett, Poundstone, Rice, Faibisch, Hunt, & Mitchell, 1996).

What Are Comprehension Skills?

Comprehension skills are the strategies a reader uses to construct meaning and retrieve information from a text. Three types of comprehension skills are recommended here: Pre-reading skills, during-reading skills, and post-reading skills (Anderson & Roit, 1996; Dole et al., 1991; Gunning, 1996). Pre-reading skills are used to activate relevant schemata, gain an overview of the information to be comprehended, and perceive the structure of the text. During-reading skills are used to develop metacognitive awareness, analyze paragraphs, and evaluate ideas gleaned from each paragraph. Post-reading skills are used to review, order, create structure, retell or explain, and evaluate information gleaned from the text. Examples of nine comprehension skills can be seen in Figure 6.9.

These skills are easily learned and can be flexibly applied to meet the demands of most reading situations. Comprehension skills must be simple and easy to use if readers are to use them. Those that are too cumbersome will not be used. Expert readers use variations of the skills described here.

How many comprehension skills do you teach? Teachers should identify and teach no more than two to five skills each year. Practice these skills throughout the curriculum. Allow students to experiment in order to find the skill that works best for them. Also effective is having students share their comprehension process in small groups.

Figure 6.9 Comprehension Skills

Comprehension Skills

Pre-Reading Comprehension Skills	During-Reading Comprehension Skills	Post-Reading Comprehension Skills
Preview - Overview 1. Look at the title and headings. 2. Read the first and last paragraph. 3. Read the article/chapter.	*Paragraph Re-Read* 1. Read each paragraph quickly. 2. Re-read to find the important ideas. 3. Continue.	*Re-Read* 1. Read the article/chapter. 2. Re-read the article/chapter. 3. Note or record important ideas.
Web and Brainstorm 1. Look at the title and headings. 2. Web and brainstorm using the topic as the central node and headings as subnodes. 3. Read the article/chapter. 4. Add to and modify the web.	*Read and Pause* 1. Read a paragraph. 2. Pause and check. (Do I understand it?) 3. Return or resume.	*Sequencing* 1. As you read the selection, list important ideas. 2. After reading, arrange in order of their importance. 3. Look for ideas of your own to add.

SUMMARY

1. Reading is learning how to use print to create meaning.
2. Scaffolded reading experiences consist of pre-reading, during-reading, and post-reading activities.
3. Thinking skills can be used to design pre- and post-reading activities for narrative and expository texts.
4. Thinking skills can be used to help students respond aesthetically to stories.
5. Comprehension skills are very much like thinking skills.
6. Teaching comprehension skills explicitly will help students improve their ability to comprehend expository text.

References

Anderson, V., & Roit, M. (1996). Linking reading comprehension instruction to language development for language-minority students. The Elementary School Journal, 96, 295-309.

Cunningham, P.M., Moore, S.A., Cunningham, J.W., & Moore, D.W. (1995). Reading and writing in elementary classrooms: Skills and observations (3rd ed.). White Plains, NY: Longman.

Cunningham, J.W., & Wall, L.K. (1994). Teaching good readers to comprehend better. Journal of Reading, 37, 480-486.

Dole, J., Duffy, G., Roehler, L., & Pearson, P.D. (1991). Moving from the old to the new: Research on reading comprehension instruction. Review of Educational Research, 61, 239-264.

Fielding, L.G., & Pearson, P.D. (1994). Reading comprehension; What works. Educational Leadership, 31, 62-68.

Fitzpatrick, K. (1994). Improving reading comprehension using critical thinking strategies. Reading Improvement, 31, 142-144.

Graves, M.F., Juel, C., & Graves, B.B. (1998). Teaching reading in the 21st century. Needham Heights, MA: Allyn and Bacon.

Gunderson, L. (1996). Reading and language development. In V. Froese (Ed.), Whole-language: Practice and theory. Needham Heights, MA: Allyn and Bacon.

Gunning, T.G. (1996). Creating reading instruction for all children. Needham Heights, MA: Allyn and Bacon.

Guther, J., Van Meter, P., McCann, A., Wigfield, A., Bennet, L., Poundstone, C., Rice, M., Failbisch, F., Hunt, B., & Mitchel, A. (1996). Growth of literacy engagement: Changes in motivations and skills during concept-oriented reading instruction. Reading Research Quarterly, 31, 306-332.

Johnson, A. (1996). Inference: A thinking skill to enhance learning and literacy. Wisconsin State Reading Association Journal, 40, 19-24.

Johnson, A., & Graves, M. (1997). Scaffolding: A tool for enhancing the reading experiences of all students. Texas Journal of Reading, 3, 23-30.

L'Engle, M. (1962). A Wrinkle in Time. New York: Bantam Doubleday Dell Books.

Ogle, D.M. (1986). KWL: A teaching model that develops active reading of expository text. The Reading Teacher, 39, 564-590.

Perkins, D.N. (1986). Thinking frames. Educational Leadership, 42, 4-10.

Reutzel, D.R., & Cooter, R.B. (1996). Teaching children to read. Englewood Cliffs, NJ: Merrill/Prentice Hall.

Rosenblatt, L.M. (1983). Literature as exploration (4th ed.). New York: Modern Language Association.

Zarillo, J. (1991). Theory becomes practice: Aesthetic teaching with literature. The New Advocate, 4, 221-234.

7

Thinking Skills and Writing

This chapter examines thinking skills as they relate to the language arts. Below are described (a) writing, (b) the process of writing, (c) poetry, (d) grammar, and (e) spelling.

WHAT IS WRITING?

Writing is a process of using print to create meaning. Its function is to transmit, create, remember, organize, or express ideas. And just like reading, writing is a constantly developing skill which improves with practice and instruction.

Writing and Speaking

Writing is more than speech written down. Because of its permanence and its one-way nature, writing is more elaborate and orderly than speech. We can write more carefully and more accurately than we can speak. Writing allows us to examine our thoughts so they can be tested, analyzed, shaped, evaluated, edited, sorted, and ordered before they are delivered. Once delivered, they become frozen in time.

Speech, however, is impermanent and is usually accompanied by a dialogue or interaction with another human. Thus, speech is comprised of shorter sentences, is less formal, and is not as organized as writing. The advantage of speech is that we can see our intended audience, judge their reaction or reception to our words, and make immediate adjustments. The disadvantage of speech is that it hangs our words out in the air without the chance to examine or retract them. Then, unless recorded, they float away like smoke.

Writing and Thinking

Writing might be more closely compared to thinking. Many authorities have commented on and investigated the relationship between thinking and writing. Scardamalia and Bereiter (1990) state that there is an integral and reciprocal relationship between the two. Freedman, Dyson, Flower, and Wallace (1987) describe writing as a process linking context and thinking. Hull (1989) portrays writing as a form of problem solving and a complex cognitive process. Elbow (1973, 1981) has long advocated making implicit cognitive processes explicit to help students write with more power, clarity, and control. Applebee (1984) describes writing as a reasoning process, a tool for rational thought, and something which improves understanding and memory of a topic. Glatthorn (1985) recommends that writing be emphasized in programs that teach thinking. Raburn and Van Schuver (1984) determined that students' thinking ability was the best predictor of success in college English composition classes. Baldwin (1991) found that journal writing resulted in significantly higher levels of student thinking, and Langer and Applebee (1987) found that writing shapes how students think.

However, writing is not the same as thinking. At the deepest level, we think in images and feelings. The words we put together can never be more than an approximation of our thoughts. Words are the colors we use to paint the flowers, but not the flowers themselves. However, the better we are at using these words, the more closely we can approximate the images and feelings we carry around inside us.

THE PROCESS OF WRITING

Writing consists of three components: (a) having ideas, (b) organizing ideas, and (c) communicating ideas. Thinking skills can be used to enhance each of these.

Having Ideas

Students must be taught how to generate ideas as part of the pre-writing process. Using the analogy of a sculptor, this pre-writing process is where the artist throws a large chunk of clay on the table. Below, four thinking skills are described which can be used in this chunk-throwing stage. These skills reflect Elbow's (1973, 1981) description of the initial steps used in effective writing in which the writer generates ideas without evaluation. Once a sufficient number of ideas have been generated, the writer can begin to shape and mold them into a coherent piece.

1. Fluency. Fluency or brainstorming is a common pre-writing strategy;

however, it cannot be assumed that students know or value this process. Thus, this skill should be modeled and taught explicitly. Sometimes it is helpful to do power-brainstorming. Here students first list as many things as they can about their writing topic in a two-minute period. Students are encouraged to keep their pencils moving at all times and quickly write the very first thing that pops into their mind without pausing to think or evaluate. Then, students trade papers with a neighbor and power-brainstorm to add still more ideas to the writing topics.

2. Web and Brainstorm. This pre-writing thinking skill helps writers to generate ideas and creates a structure to use to carry those ideas. With older students, each subtopic or node of the web can become a heading for a different section of their paper. With younger writers, each subtopic or node can become a paragraph. The visual aspect of the web allows writers to see the structure of the whole and the relationship of the different parts.

3. Creative Problem Solving. For narrative writing: (a) identify a problem, (b) generate ideas for a solution, (c) pick a solution, (d) create characters and a beginning, and (e) revise and refine (see Figure 7.1). For expository writing: (a) identify a real life problem or need, (b) generate ideas to find the best solution, then (c) provide evidence or reasoning to support the solution.

4. Supporting a Statement. Writers make a statement or a claim initially, then provide evidence or reasoning to support their statement.

Organizing Ideas

After generating ideas, effective writers begin to examine them, searching for meaningful patterns and organizing them into groups (Elbow, 1991; Rico, 1989). Organizing skills are designed to help facilitate the identification of patterns and the creation of groups. Here, the artist takes the chunk of clay and begins to shape it so that it has the desired effect. As the emerging work evolves, artists and writers begin to perceive the structure and the relationships between ideas. Oftentimes this process leads to the generation of more ideas. Below are two thinking skills used to help writers bring order to their thoughts and perceptions.

1. Creating Groups. This is the most common thinking skill used for organizing expository writing. Here, writers examine their notes, look for emerging patterns, and then arrange their ideas into groups. These groups become paragraphs, headings for different sections, or chapters.

2. Ordering. After all relevant data are collected, writers organize them from most important to least important, biggest to smallest, or chronologically. Using these types of organizational patterns will help readers understand the text.

Communicating Ideas

Communicating ideas is the step where writers are concerned with how the writing might play inside the head of the reader. Here, the overall effect as well as mechanical elements are attended to. It is like the sculptor putting the final touches on the clay sculpture.

Figure 7.1 CPS for Generating Story Ideas

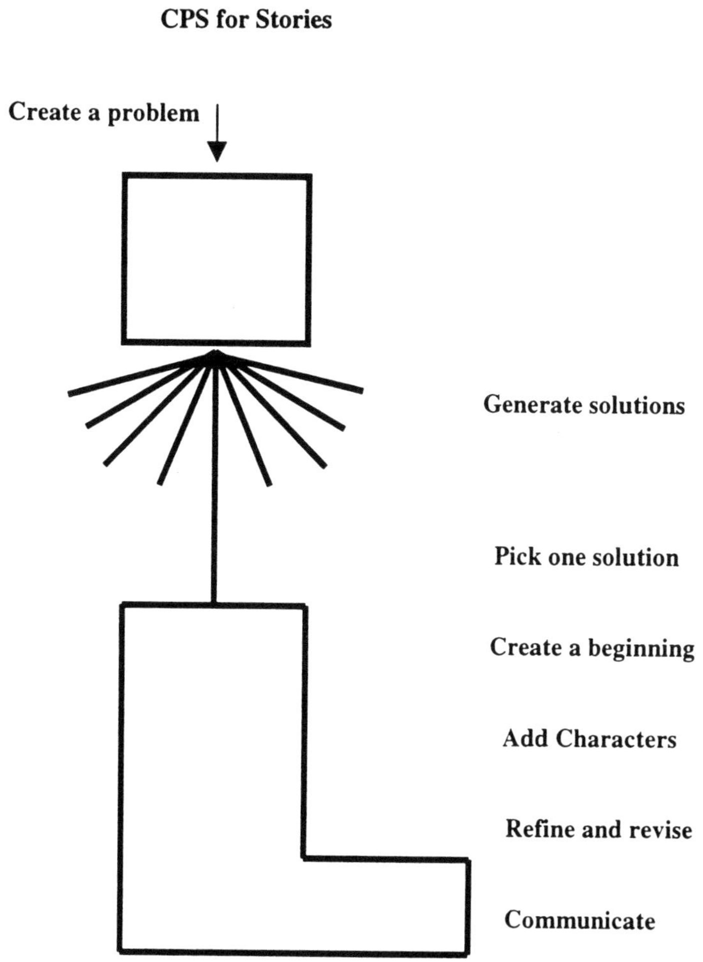

CPS for Stories

Create a problem

Generate solutions

Pick one solution

Create a beginning

Add Characters

Refine and revise

Communicate

---

1. Elaboration. As writers re-read and revise, they examine and assess their work in order to improve or embellish it. How can the sentence be crisper, more concise, more descriptive, or most expressive? How might the language make the scene come alive? How can understanding be improved? How can the paragraphs be arranged to provide the reader with maximum impact?

2. Generate Relationships. Elbow (1981) encourages writers to find relationships in order to create metaphors, similes, and analogies. These enhance the reader's understanding by connecting new ideas to known ideas.

Evaluating Writing

A rubric is a set of criteria for a piece of work that describes the quality of the piece. Here, students generate the criteria for an effective story or piece of writing, then evaluate their work based on this criteria. The rubric can serve to guide students as they write. The thinking skill *Evaluation/Critique* is used here. An example of a rubric is shown below (see Figure 7.2). You can also let students determine the criteria for effective writing.

Figure 7.2   General Scoring Rubric for Writing

Rubrics for Writing

	3	2	1
accomplishment of task	successful	reasonably successful	not successful
organization	logical, focused, clear	some flaws; may lack focus	confusing; no organization
sentence structure	correct	some errors, limited variety	many errors; lacks variety
vocabulary	clear, precise, expressive	appropriate; not vivid, precise, or expressive	limited; unsuitable
mechanics	few significant errors	several errors	many significant errors

POETRY

Poetry is the process of using words to paint a picture. It is a composition in verse that varies in form. Like an arrangement of flowers in a vase, poetry is an arrangement of words that uses metaphors, similes, memories, and feelings to create an image. It is also an effective tool for advancing children's language skills as it calls for careful observation and a precise use of words. Writers of poetry must be attuned to patterns, sounds, rhythms, and the subtle effect of words.

Form Versus Function

Teachers should rarely insist that children use a particular poetry form to express their ideas. This robs the writer. The form of poetry is merely a tool used to express ideas. It is the hammer that pounds the nail, not the nail. The haiku is perhaps the greatest villain here. From an adult perspective, this is a seemingly easy form to teach and learn, but from children's perspective it is an abstraction found outside the child that gets in the way of expressing thoughts. Using the haiku, children must not only attend to their ideas, but also to words and the limitations of a particular form. The form, then, becomes more important than the function, which is to express ideas. Instead, expose children to many forms or styles of poetry and allow them to make choices of form and style.

Creating Poems

Reading poems aloud every day will get students ready to create their own poems. Also, teachers can encourage risk-taking and creativity by writing and sharing their own poems with students.

The poem starter (Figure 7.3) can be used to get poems started initially. This is comprised of five steps: First, students find a writing topic. Second, they brainstorm to generate ideas for things that are seen, heard, or felt relative to their writing topic. Third, students look for similarities to other things in order to create metaphors and similes. Fourth, students organize their ideas. Finally, students read their poems aloud, experimenting with the sounds of words and sentences in order to find more effective or more descriptive ways of saying things.

Figure 7.3 Poem Starting for Creating Poetry

Poem Starter

I. Topic: Start with a thought. Use semantic webbing to create a number of different ideas to find your topic.

II. Texture: Using your topic, fill in the chart below

I hear ...	
I see ...	
I feel ...	
I taste ...	
I smell ...	
Just like ...	

Poetry Forms or Techniques

The five steps of the poem starter and their related thinking skills can be used with the seven poetry forms described below. However, these forms are simply ways of organizing ideas. Students should be encouraged to choose poetry forms or writing techniques which are best suited to their ideas and to their way of thinking.

1. Free Verse. Teach this form first whenever studying poetry. The beauty of this form is that it has no required form. Words, verse, punctuation, and capitalization are all chosen by the poet for their particular effect.

Example: After going for my daily run, I sat in the locker room before taking a shower and listened. I created the following free verse poem.

The College Locker Room
Large,
Rows, and rows of metal lockers.
Benches held in place by firm steel girders.
Order.

Symmetry.
All is right in this universe.

Humanity enters.
Voices talking now.
Showers splash water in echoing chambers.
The smell of competition and sweaty clothes permeates.
The locker room smell.
Disinfectant.
Words bounce merrily from one end to another.
Talk of games and running and exercise.
Behind a cage,
old men pass out towels and repair football helmets.

2. *Alliteration.* Alliteration is the repetition of words with similar beginning sounds, or words with similar consonant sounds anywhere in them. Here, students (a) begin with a writing topic, (b) generate words with similar sounds, then (c) organize their words to create an image or feeling. Example: As part of a second grade unit in science, I wanted my class to help me create a poem about seashells. I put this word on the board and had students help me generate words that begin with "s" and "sh.". They came up with the following: swim, shine, shapes, shoes, sloppy, sharp, slippery, seal, shore, shiny, ship, sunshine, and silk. Next, I thought out loud and used the overhead to begin creating ideas or sentences which used as many of the new words as possible. I played with some ideas and created a very rough first draft (sloppy copy) of a poem. The next day, I shared a revised draft of my poem with my students and let them begin creating their own poems.

Seashells
Shiny.
Stuck in the silky sand,
like chocolate chips in a cookie.
Shapes,
along the shore,
sharp and round.
Seashells.

My undergraduate students were feeling the stress of midterm exams. I decided to create a poem about stress and tests. As a class, we generated words that had the "t" or "st" sounds in them and came up with the following: stingy, lost, bust, stupid, terrible, tough, mess, touchy, stop, and pest. Again, I used some of these words to create my first draft. The following day I shared my poem.

> **Tests**
> *Tests.*
> *Tests are terrible.*
> *They are tough.*
> *I am touchy*
> *when I take them.*
> *They can be trouble.*
> *I am a mess with stress.*
> *You need time*
> *to use your mind*
> *and study.*
> *Tests.*

3. Assonance. Assonance is the repetition of words that have similar vowel sounds. It was the beginning of June and I was finishing a unit on reptiles in my second grade science class. I decided to play with the sounds of the word, "June" and try to include a reptile. Our class generated the following list of words: tune, move, moon, poodle, blooper, soup, soon, loop, turtle, few, and burnt. The following poem ensued:

> **Turtle**
> *In June I was walking and whistling a*
> *tune, tune, tune.*
> *Ooooo! I saw him*
> *move.*
> *A turtle.*
> *Beautiful.*
> *"Soon," I thought,*
> *"You*
> *will be on my*
> *spoon as turtle*
> *soup."*

4. Onomatopoeia. This is where a writer forms words by imitating sounds. Here, students (a) think of an event or situation, (b) generate a list of actions related to that situation, (c) ascribe sounds to each action, then (d) organize their ideas and sounds.

> **Mosquito**
> *Zzzzzz.*

I sleep peacefully.
Bzzzzzzz.
A little intruder comes.
Plt.
He lightly lands on my arm.
Zoink!
He jabs me with his stinger.
Slurp!
He sips my blood.
Smash!
He is no more.

5. Repetition. In using repetition, the writer looks for words, phrases, or sentences to repeat.

Morning Goodness!
My ears assaulted.
   Alarm clock, SCREECH!!!.
My eyes pried open.
   Creeeeeeeeeeeak.
My feet hit the floor.
   Thud ... thud.
My head is empty.
   Echo, echo, echo ...
My veins are screaming,
   Coffee! Coffee! Coffee!
My goodness,
   I hate morning.

6. Persona. To use this, writers speak in the voice of an object or animal, rather than through their own voice. This is an effective way to integrate science and the arts as students use their knowledge to imagine the life of an animal or object.

Rock
I sit all day minding my own business.
I don't say naughty things.
I don't tease anybody.
But people walk on me.
And sometimes little boys
throw me at cows.

7. Personification. This technique asks the poet to give human qualities to nonhuman things. *Comparing* and *Generating Relationships* are two thinking skills that help students produce ideas.

> ***Rocket***
> *A rocket sits on the pad.*
> *Sleeping peacefully.*
> *All of a sudden, it come to life.*
> *It grumbles and rumbles angrily.*
> *It blasts and bellows*
> *It screams and jumps into the air,*
> *off, off, off .... into space*
> *to quietly watch the stars.*

GRAMMAR AND THINKING SKILLS

Grammar is a study of the way our language works. It is also a system of rules describing sentence structure and work usage. However, studying grammar in isolation (apart from authentic writing tasks) replicates the stand-alone approach described in Chapter 3 and does little to improve the quality of students' writing (Hillocks, 1986; Western, 1978), or guarantee that they are able to use the particular grammar skills under real writing conditions (Graves, 1983). Bromely (1988) found no relationship between the teaching of grammar in isolation and the quality of written compositions. Instead, time spent composing has a more positive effect on students' ability to use grammar correctly and to form and organize their ideas. This is not to imply that grammar should not be taught; rather, grammar skills should be taught using short mini-lessons in the context of authentic writing tasks. This way of teaching grammar replicates the embedded approach described in Chapter 3.

Traditional Grammar

Traditional grammar instruction involves identifying various parts of speech and then learning the rules for putting the parts together (Block, 1997). Below, four thinking skills are described which can be used with this approach.

1. Analyze. Here, students examine sentences and describe them in terms of their component parts.

2. Creating Groups. Using this thinking skill, students (a) examine the words found in a page, paragraph, or passage; (b) look for common themes, recurring patterns, or groups; and then (c) arrange the words into groups. Results can be recorded in a learning log. This activity can be extended by having students graph their findings or use these groups to compare the writing to another piece of writing of similar length (see *Compare and Contrast* below).

3. Investigation. Once students have a common vocabulary for word categories (nouns, verbs, adjectives, adverbs, etc.), this thinking skill can be used to answer questions about word usage and sentence design. These questions might include: What kinds of words are found most often? How long is the sentence? What kinds of words are found in each sentence? How many words per adjectives (WPA), words per verb (WPV), or words per noun (WPN) does the author use? Is there a particular word order that is found most often in sentences? Or, is the topic sentence generally found at the beginning, middle, or end of the paragraph?

4. Compare and Contrast. As an inquiry project, have students analyze a fifty or hundred word segment of writing by a favorite author. They record the categories or types of words (adjectives, nouns, adverbs, etc.), and the number of words found in each category. These data can be used to make comparisons to other works by the same author, other works by different authors, other parts of the book, or other types of books. Students might also determine if the overall effect of the passage contributed to different types of words being used. For example: When authors are creating exciting passages, sad passages, or funny passages, are there certain types of words or sentences that are common to each?

Transformational-Generative Grammar Instruction

This approach to grammar instruction looks at what we do when we create, change, or invent sentences (Block, 1997). Transformational-generative grammar proposes that sentences have two levels: deep structure and surface structure. Deep structure is the most basic meaning of a sentence. This meaning can be represented in several forms which are the surface structure.

1. Flexibility. Have students imagine a picture of a black dog (deep structure). Individually, each student describes the image in his or her journal using one sentence (surface structure). Their sentences are written on the board and the variety of sentences is compared. Next, students generate other possibilities so that they can see the wide variety of possible sentences. To extend this activity, students take a sentence from a piece of their writing. In pairs or small groups, they describe this sentence in terms of its most basic component (deep structure). Then, they generate as many possible ways to express this sentence as they can. Seeing a variety of ways to transform deep structure into surface structure sentences helps students better understand grammar.

2. Elaboration. Students use this thinking skill to embellish sentences in order to create different effects. For example, using the sentence, *"The boy ran down the street,"* ask students to make this more interesting, mysterious, exciting, funny, descriptive, longer, shorter, or make it related to school in some way.

Sentence Combining

This approach to grammar instruction seeks to raise students' intuitive knowledge of grammar to a conscious level (Block, 1997). Here, students choose two sentence from their own writing and combine them using as few words as possible while still retaining clarity and the original meaning of both sentences. This leads to discussion and instruction related to commas, prepositions, verbs, adverbs, and conjunctions.

SPELLING

Traditional approaches to spelling instruction rely on students memorizing a list of words each week. However, words studied out of context are of minimal effect in helping students develop spelling proficiency and worse, they keep students away from real writing experiences (Gentry & Gilbert, 1993; Graves, 1983). This section looks at how thinking skills can be used to enhance students' ability to spell correctly.

Spelling Proficiency and Visual Memory

What is the difference between a good speller and a poor speller? Gentry and Gilbert (1993) suggest that spelling proficiency might be attributed to one's visual memory capacity. According to this theory, good spellers are better able to store and retrieve necessary letter patterns from long term memory. Effective spelling instruction then should be aimed at improving the efficiency of cognitive storage and retrieval by helping students becoming more aware of letter patterns and word parts. Thus, only a small amount of direct instruction covering a few spelling rules and the most common prefixes, suffixes, and word families is needed (Topping, 1995).

Word Class

Word class combines thinking skills instruction with a self-selected approach to spelling instruction and can be adapted for use in Grades 2 through 12 (Johnson, 1997). A self-selected approach to spelling teaches students how to generate and choose the words they will study each week (Graves, 1983; Scott,

1994; Topping, 1995). This choice might happen in one of three ways:

1. Choice within a topic. Given a topic, students create their own spelling lists. Words are taken from topics studied in science, social studies, or literature units.

2. Choice within a letter pattern. Given a spelling pattern, students create their own lists. Here, the teacher begins with a short mini-lesson covering a particular spelling pattern or skill. Then students work with a partner to create a list of words using that particular letter pattern or skill.

3. Total choice. Students use their lives and experience to create their own spelling lists. This approach is usually the most interesting, as children search their lives for interesting and meaningful words.

A word wall (Cunningham & Allington, 1994), can be used to call attention to interesting or important words within the given topic or spelling pattern. To insure that students are exposed to words of varying difficulty levels, a teacher may choose to include two to five mandatory words for all students to study each week. However, Topping (1995) found that the words students choose are usually longer and more complex than those chosen by teachers.

There are four advantages of using the self-selected approach: (a) students' ideas and experiences are valued, (b) more time can be spent doing real writing, (c) money spent on consumable spelling books can be used to buy real books, and (d) students are able to add depth and dimension to their word knowledge.

Word Class Weekly Schedule

Spelling instruction should be limited to approximately 20 minutes a day (Gentry & Gilbert, 1993). The following weekly schedule uses four thinking skills to provide eight different activities. These skills add depth and dimension to word knowledge, highlight letter patterns, enhance writing skills, teach general thinking skills, and value students' ideas and experiences.

Monday

1. Fluency. Working in large group or with a partner, students brainstorm to generate 8-15 words to use for their spelling lists. After they have selected words for their lists, students check the correct spelling and record them in a word journal or learning log. For example, a sixth grade class was studying space in science class. In large group, students generated a list of 25 space words while the teacher recorded them on the board. Each student then chose 10 words to study that week. One student selected the following words: space, rocket, planet, oxygen, gravity, life, universe, moon, atmosphere, launch.

Tuesday - Thursday

Working individually or with a partner, students use thinking skills for the following activities.

2. Fluency and *Originality.* Here, students brainstorm to create a group of descriptive words or associations to go with one or more of their list words. These associating words are used to write a descriptive paragraph. For example, if the topic was space, a spelling list word might be "launch". Words, thoughts, or images associated with this word are take-off, smoke, noise, rumble, power, liftoff, launch pad, fire, or push. Many of these words can then be used to describe a rocket launch.   Below is a sample of such a paragraph written by a sixth grade student.

A launch is when a rocket takes off into space. The rocket is fired into space from a launch pad. It is powered by powerful rocket engines. Thick smoke and loud noise erupt as the rocket pushes away from earth (Joey, age 12).

Allow students time to share their creations in large or small group settings. At the end of the lesson, they should record their best or most interesting paragraphs in their word journal.

3. Web and Brainstorm to write. Here, students use webbing and brainstorming to generate ideas based on one or more spelling words (Figure 7.4). The web provides structure to a piece of writing while generating information about a topic. Each node becomes a paragraph. At the end of the lesson, students record their writing in their word journal.

4. Web and Brainstorm to speak. Students pick a word from their spelling list to use in creating a short one-minute oral presentation. Working with a partner, students web and brainstorm to provide information and ideas related to this list word for their oral presentation. A web provides the structure to help students communicate more effectively.

5. Webbing to find related word parts. Here, students use webbing and brainstorming to find related parts of a word. Students choose a word from their spelling list and break it into beginning, middle, and ending parts. For example the word "space" can be broken into three parts: (a) "sp" beginning, (b) long "a" middle, and (c) "ce" ending (Figure 7.5). The word "space" is the central idea. "Sp", "long a", and "ce" are the three nodes. With a partner, students brainstorm on each node to find words with similar parts. The web is recorded in students' word journal.

6. Creating Groups. Students use *Creating Groups* to organize their spelling words into groups. Groups can be created based on spelling patterns or ideas (see Figure 7.6). This should be modeled many times in a large group

Figure 7.4 A Web to Generate Ideas for Writing

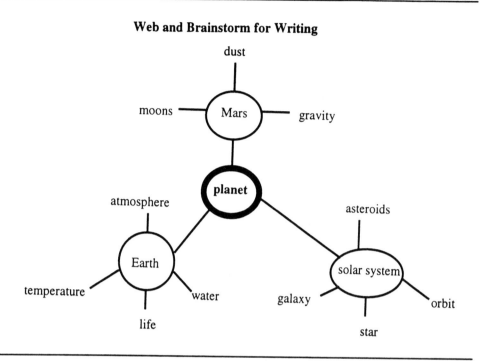

Web and Brainstorm for Writing

setting before students do it in small groups. At the end of the lesson, students will describe and record their lists using their new groups.

7. Comparing. Here, students look for similarities between words related to ideas or letter patterns. Students use the Compare-O-Graph (see Figure 7.7) to compare five words at a time. Students record their Compare-O-Graphs in their word journal.

Friday

On Friday, students work with a partner to take their weekly spelling test. Each partner gives the test to the other. Results are recorded, along with reflections or observations, after the spelling test is completed.

Figure 7.5 A Web to Find Related Word Parts

Web and Brainstorm for Word Parts

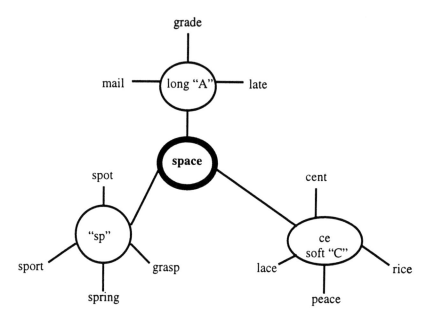

Assessment

The results of these weekly spelling tests can be recorded in students' spelling journals. Students might also chart their progress by graphing the results in their writing portfolio. However, I recommend a more authentic and accurate form of spelling assessment called WPH (words-per-hundred) scores. Here, the teacher examines a student's final draft of an edited piece, designates a 100-word segment, and counts the number of words spelled correctly in that 100-word segment to arrive at a WPH score. This is a more accurate reflection of spelling ability under authentic writing conditions. Also, this is how a writer's spelling ability is evaluated in the real world. With younger students, a WPF (words-per-fifty) score can be used.

Figure 7.6 Compare-O-Graphs for Spelling Patterns and Ideas

Creating Groups

Spelling Pattern Groups	List: space, rocket, planet, oxygen, gravity, life, universe, moon, atmosphere, launch
1. Ending e-consonant group:	rocket, planet, oxygen, atmosphere.
2. Final e group:	space, life, universe, atmosphere.
3. Double consonant group:	space, rocket, planet, atmosphere, launch.
4. Consonant blend group:	space, planet, gravity, atmosphere, launch.
5. Three-syllable group:	oxygen, gravity, universe, atmosphere.

Idea Groups	List: space, rocket, planet, oxygen, gravity, life, universe, moon, atmosphere, launch
1. Spaceship group:	rocket, launch.
2. Planet group:	moon, atmosphere, gravity, planet.
3. Huge group:	space, universe.
4. Earth group:	planet, oxygen, gravity, life, moon, atmosphere.
5. Invisible group:	space, oxygen, gravity.

Figure 7.7 A Compare-O-Graph

Compare-O-Graph

Spelling List: space, rocket, planet, oxygen, gravity, life, universe, moon, atmosphere, launch.

	rocket	planet	oxygen	gravity
SPACE	- e. - double consonant. - 2 vowels. - 3 consonants. - a rocket travels in space.	- e. - a. - consonant blend. - 2 vowels. - a planet is in space.	- e. - no oxygen in space.	- a. - 2 vowels. - consonant blend. - no gravity in space.

SUMMARY

1. Writing is the process of using print to create meaning.
2. Writing consists of three processes: having ideas, organizing, and communicating ideas.
3. Poetry is a composition in verse that uses words to paint a picture.
4. Grammar is best learned in the context of real writing and composing tasks.
5. Traditional approaches to spelling instruction are of little use in helping students spell under real writing conditions.
6. Thinking skills can be used with a self-selected approach to create a more student-centered approach to spelling instruction.

References

Adams, M.J., (1992) <u>Beginning to read</u>. Cambridge, MA: MIT Press.

Atwell, N. (1987). <u>In the middle: Writing, reading and learning with adolescents</u>. Upper Montclair, NJ: Boynton/Cook Publishers, Inc.

Bartch, J. (1992). An alternative to spelling: An integrated approach. <u>Language Arts, 69</u>, 404-408.

Butler, S. (1996). The writing connection. In V. Froese (Ed.). <u>Whole language: Practice and theory</u>. Boston, MA: Allyn and Bacon.

Clark, L.K. (1988). Invented versus traditional spelling in first graders' writing: Effects on learning to spell and read. <u>Research in the Teaching of English, 22</u>, 281-309.

Cunningham, P.M., & Allington, R.L. (1994). <u>Classrooms that work: They can all read and write</u>. New York: HarperCollins.

Cunningham, P.M., Moore, S.A., Cunningham, J.W., & Moore, S.W. (1995). <u>Reading and writing in elementary classrooms: Strategies and observations</u>. White Plains, NY: Longman.

Edwards, J. (1985). Spelling corrections alter children's voices. <u>Highway One: Canadian Journal of Language Education, 8</u>, 6-14.

Gentry, R.L., & Gilbert, J.W. (1993). <u>Teaching kids to spell</u>. Portsmouth, NH: Heinemann.

Glatthorn, A.A. (1985). Thinking and writing. In F. Link (Ed.), <u>Essays on the intellect</u>. Alexandria, VA: Association for the Supervision of Curriculum Development.

Graves, D. (1983). <u>Writing: Teachers and children at work</u>. Portsmouth, NH: Heinemann.

Gunderson, L., & Shapiro, J. (1987). Some findings on whole language instruction. <u>Reading-Canada-Lecture, 5</u>, 22-26.

Froese, V. (1996). <u>Whole language: Theory and practice</u>. Boston, MA: Allyn and Bacon.

Johnson, A. (1998). Word class: A way to modify spelling instruction for gifted learners. <u>The Roeper Review, 20</u>, 128-131.

Johnson, A. (1996). Inference: A thinking skill to enhance learning and literacy. <u>Wisconsin State Reading Association Journal, 40</u>, 9-13.

Perkins, D.N. (1986). Thinking frames. <u>Educational Leadership, 42</u>, 4-10.

Perkins, D.N. (1987). Thinking frames: An integrative perspective on teaching cognitive skills. In J.B. Baron & R.J. Sternberg (Eds.), <u>Teaching thinking skills: Theory and practice</u> (pp. 41-61). New York: W.H. Freeman.

Robinson, R.D., McKenna, M.C., & Wedman, J.M. (1996). <u>Trends in literacy</u>. Boston, MA: Allyn and Bacon.

Scott, J.E. (1994). Spelling for readers and writers. <u>The Reading Teacher, 48</u>, 188-190.

Topping, K. (1995). Cued spelling: A powerful technique for parent and peer tutoring. <u>The Reading Teacher, 48</u>, 374-385.

Weaver, C. (1990). <u>Understanding whole language</u>. Portsmouth, NH: Heinemann.

8

Thinking Skills and Science

This chapter examines three areas related to science and thinking skills: (a) science as a verb, (b) inquiry, and (c) thinking in science class.

SCIENCE IS A VERB

One of the most basic human instincts is the drive to make sense of the world around us. This is the essence of science, the process of which has been going on in various forms long before there were words or written languages to record it. Science is not solely a body of knowledge or a particular content area, but a way of seeing, a process used to examine and organize our environment. Science, therefore, is a verb. To science: to look, ask questions, test questions, create order from chaos, find answers, and develop concepts.

Knowledge

While science is not a body of knowledge, it is highly dependent on having a well-organized knowledge base (Armbruster, 1993; Gallagher & Gallagher, 1994; Hodson, 1988; Thelen, 1984). Knowledge helps the scientist structure and assimilate new information. Science experiments are built upon accepted theories and previous research. New data make sense only when they are grounded in what is familiar. Thus, methods of science involve generating relations between the prior knowledge and new knowledge.

What Scientists Do

Scientists are simply those who ask questions and find answers. In fact, we all "science" in some way each day. Our questions might be as grand as, "How did our universe begin?" or as mundane as, " Which line at the grocery store checkout is faster?" or "I wonder what kind of response my new haircut will generate?" Teachers "science" when they ask questions such as: "How will this new teaching technique work?" or "How are Sally's reading skills coming along?" or "How can I help Billy learn long division?"

Gallagher and Gallagher (1994) list seven essential activities of a scientist. A scientist: (a) develops content expertise, (b) detects problems or asks questions, (c) observes, (d) organizes and classifies data, (e) measures, (f) hypothesizes, and (g) experiments. In the classroom, these seven activities could be applied to almost any subject area to create an effective science unit.

INQUIRY IS SCIENCE

Inquiry is when the scientific method is applied to a learning situation (Savage & Armstrong, 1996). More specifically, it is the process of designing learning activities which incorporate methods of science. There is not one scientific method; rather, there are many methods of science which are used to ask and answer questions (Hodson, 1988). Three of the thinking skills described in this book are examples of these: (a) *Creating Groups,* (b) *Investigation,* and (c) *Experimenting.*

Creating Groups

This thinking skill reflects naturalistic or ethnographic methodologies often used in education. Here the scientist observes a field or an event in order to understand it. As the data are collected and recorded, they are organized into groups. Finally, the scientist describes the field or event in terms of the groups.

Activities for Creating Groups
1. The gerbil observation. Here, a small group of students observe a gerbil's behavior for ten minutes and record specific gerbil behaviors. These behaviors are then put into four to six categories or groups. Example: running, digging, chewing, and drinking. The next day, the categories are used as headings and a data retrieval chart (DRC) is constructed to help students gather and organize information (see Figure 8.1). A DRC is any graphic organizer which helps students gather and organize information. Initially, the teacher prepares these for students; however, students will eventually be able to create their own DRCs.

Using the DRC, students observe the gerbil for a given amount of time and put a tally mark in the appropriate category every time each behavior is displayed.

This information is used to create a graph or table which describes the type and frequency of gerbil behavior. This activity can be extended by comparing gerbil behaviors at different times of the day, comparing one gerbil to another, or comparing gerbil behavior to the behavior of another animal. Another extension is to use this same process to observe a group of students during recess.

2. The story. After reading a story or a chapter, students brainstorm to create a list of important or memorable events. Next, the list is analyzed and the events put into groups. The number of events in each group is recorded. These data can also be displayed in graph or table form. To extend this activity, use the data to compare one chapter to another, one book to another, or one author to another.

Figure 8.1 DRC for Recording Behaviors

Animal: gerbil

Behavior ➜	running	digging	chewing	drinking

3. Plot of land. Working in pairs, students are assigned a one-foot-square plot of land outside. Their square is designated by putting a piece of yard around the perimeter. The pair's first task is to carefully observe their piece of land and describe it using words and diagrams in a learning log. Then students note and record the types of things found on their land. Categories are formed such as plant life, rocks, soil, signs of animal life, or signs of human life. The number of items in each category is recorded. (You may want to use land that is not too grassy.) These data are displayed in graph or table form. This activity is extended by comparing land in various areas or using the square to estimate the number of rocks or blades of grass in a large area.

4. Rocks. This activity is effective in helping primary students begin to learn about scientific methods. Here, students bring in three to five interesting rocks. In groups of two to four, students combine their rocks to create a collection. Next, the collection is analyzed and groups or categories of rocks are formed. Finally, the collection is described in terms of the categories. These results can be described using graphs or tables. To extend this activity, one collection can be compared to another using similar categories.

Investigation

This type of inquiry is highly dependent on first asking or identifying a question. The scientist then becomes a detective who investigates to find data or clues to answer the question.

Activities for Investigation

An example of this would be to ask students, "What kind of movie do students in our grade prefer?" Data could be collected two different ways. First, a small group of student-scientists could ask individuals to name one of their favorite movies. These answers are recorded. When all responses are in, student-scientists look at the list, create groups, and use tally marks to indicate the number of movies in each group. This is an example of an open-ended question. While these types of questions are more cumbersome to analyze and organize, the answers tend to be more accurate.

The second method would be to create a DRC which had the categories already prepared (see Figure 8.2). Here, the student-scientists simply ask

Figure 8.2 DRC for the Movie Inquiry

Inquiry Question: What type of movie do 5th grade students prefer?

Comedy		Action		Horror		Drama	
male	female	male	female	male	female	male	female

---

individuals to name a favorite category. Tally marks are used to record the number of responses in each category. These data are quantified and communicated by using a table or graph. This inquiry can be extended by comparing females to males, older students to younger students, or adults to children.

Other types of inquiry questions include the following: Which flavor of ice cream is most popular? What is the most popular sport to play? What do most students do on Saturday? What kind of shoes do most people wear? What color are most of the birds in a given area? What kinds of TV shows are most popular? What radio station is most popular? What type of music do must students enjoy? Where do birds sit? What kinds of trees are found on the playground? What kinds of non-human animal life can be observed outside? How many different kinds of plants are on the school grounds? How many rocks are found in a square foot of the playground? How many rocks are on the whole playground? How is the ground on the north side of the school different than the ground on the south side of the school?

Experimenting

This type of inquiry is what is most often associated with the scientific method. The only difference between this and *Investigation* is that *Experimenting* has a test or procedure which is run in order to answer a question. This type of inquiry is also highly dependent on first having identified a question.

Activities for Experimenting

1. Flammable substances. For younger students, the question is, "Which is more flammable: plastic or cork?" Here, the teacher exposes each to fire while students observe. Their observations and descriptions are recorded in their learning logs along with diagrams or illustrations.

To extend this with older students, the question is, "Which substances are most flammable?" Equal amounts of four substances (plastic, cork, wood, paper), are exposed to fire. Each substance is timed to see how long it takes for the fire to consume it. The question might also be, "Which substance produces the highest flame?" Again, expose equal amounts of various substances to a flame. Students use a measuring stick to record the height of the flame at its highest point. This calls for students to use measuring and observation skills. The question might again be, "How do the flame and smoke differ for each substance?" Or, "Is there any relationship between the height of the flame and the time it took to burn? Is there any relationship between the type of smoke and the time it took to burn?"

Students will often want to extend this experiment by testing other substances. This is what science is about and as long as they are observing and recording, this should be encouraged. Students will also begin to discuss concepts related to validity and reliability as they discover that each object needs to be held in the same fixed position in order to have a fair test.

   2. The gerbil observation. The gerbil observation described above can be turned into an experiment simply by asking the question first, then designing a specific method to answer this question. Example: What are the differences between gerbil behavior and mouse behavior? The experiment would be to watch each for a ten-minute period and use a DRC to record their behaviors.

   3. Gerbil paths. When left alone on a table top, what path does a gerbil take? Does this path change over time? Get a large piece of butcher paper and a crayon. Draw a small circle in the middle of the butcher paper. Set a gerbil down in the circle and observe its movement for 20 seconds. Then pick up the gerbil and use the crayon to draw its path on the butcher paper. (Students might prefer to record the gerbil's path on a separate piece of paper.) Repeat this process several times making sure the gerbil is facing the same direction at the start. Students will describe how the gerbil's path changes and offer ideas as to why.

   4. Where's the raisin? "How long does it take for a gerbil to learn where a raisin is?" Put a piece of butcher paper on the table and draw a small circle on both ends. Put a hungry gerbil in one circle and a raisin in the other. Using a stopwatch, time how long it takes the gerbil to find the raisin (do not let the gerbil eat the raisin). Repeat this several times to see if the time decreases. These data are displayed on a line graph. This experiment can be extended by comparing one gerbil to another or one species (hamster, white mice) to another.

Elements of Inquiry

   True inquiry contains the following three elements: knowledge, structure, and freedom.

Knowledge
   Background knowledge is supplied by the teacher so that the inquiry question can be put in context. For example, if an inquiry activity is designed related to American cities (Figure 8.3), students must first be provided with a certain amount of background knowledge about cities before they are given an inquiry question. Without this element, the inquiry is simply a matter of learning-by-guessing. A well-organized knowledge base helps guide the process of data retrieval and analysis.

Figure 8.3 DRC for Inquiry Activity Related to Cities

Inquiry Question: What are the similarities and differences of major United States cities?

Cities ↓	Climate	Population	Major Industries	Latitude and Longitude
Boston				
Chicago				
New Orleans				
Miami				
Los Angeles				

Structure

Structure is used to guide students as they learn how to ask questions, answer questions, and communicate their answers. In the beginning stages of inquiry, the teacher asks the majority of questions; however, students eventually learn how to ask their own questions. DRCs are used to provide structure when collecting data in the form of a DRC. An example of a DRC used for a social studies inquiry can be seen in Figure 8.4.

Lab reports are used to prove structure when reporting inquiry results. A lab report helps students communicate their ideas and can be used with any type of inquiry in any subject area. Figure 8.6 shows an example of a lab report used in a social studies inquiry. The lab report consists of three parts:

Conditions. This describes the inquiry question; what went on before the experiment, observation, or inquiry; and how students gathered information.

Results. Just the facts are described here. Students tell exactly what happened or describes the data collected using as few words as possible. If students are doing an inquiry which uses numerical information, graphs, charts, and tables can be used here.

Ideas. Here students add their ideas, tell what the data might mean, or describe how it could be used.

Figure 8.4 DRC for a Social Studies Inquiry

Inquiry Question: What lifestyle changes have occurred in the last 60 years?

Change Over Time

Time Period ↓	Music	Types of Transportation	Energy to Heat Houses	Hair Styles
Today				
1970's				
1950's				
1930's				

Freedom

The last element of inquiry is freedom. If it is true inquiry, all answers must be accepted as long there are data to support them. A good inquiry activity does not lead students to predetermined answers.

The Inquiry Process

In the classroom, the inquiry process starts when a teacher or student asks a question. Questions might include: What makes a good friend? What things make the loudest noise when hit? What kind of bridge will hold the most weight? Or what things do major US cities have in common? Next, students gather data. Finally, the data are organized and used to answer the original question.

Figure 8.5 shows an example of an inquiry lesson based around the question, What is a hero? The input section of the lesson provides knowledge related to heroes. A DRC is used during the activity section to help students gather and organize their thinking. A lab report is used to help students communicate their ideas (Figure 8.6).

Figure 8.5 An inquiry Lesson Plan

Grade: 4

OBJECTIVE: Students will learn about heroes.

INTRODUCTION: Kurt Vonnegut, Kirby Pucket, my father, and Jimmy Carter are some of my heroes or people I look up to.

INPUT:

1. Heroes are people we look up to.
2. They have some trait or talent that we think is important.
 A. We would like to have this same trait or talent.
3. For example: Kurt Vonnegut is a very creative writer (picture, book).
 A. Kirby Pucket always trained hard and played hard (pictures).
 B. Katherine Pattersen writes great books that are very touching (pictures, books).
 C. Jimmy Carter was a president who stood up for what he believed. He tries to help people make their lives better (pictures, magazine articles).
 D. My father was my hero (picture). He always worked hard, respected people, and supported me.
4. Heroes can be famous and not famous.
5. Heroes are perfect. Nobody's perfect.
 A. They are just humans who have a trait or talent that we think is important or valuable.

ACTIVITY:

1. Inquiry question: What is a hero? What qualities do heroes have in common?
2. In small group, find four heroes that are familiar to all or most.
3. Brainstorm to generate traits or experiences of each hero.
4. Use the data retrieval chart to list and organize ideas.
5. Each small group describes its general conclusions.
6. Individually, students write their conclusion in their learning log.

Data Retrieval Chart

Hero ➡	Ken Griffey Jr.	Sheryle Swoops	Martina Hingus	Gary Paulsen
Traits or experiences ➡				

Conclusions:

Figure 8.6 A Lab Report for an Inquiry Lesson.

Lab Report

Conditions

Our group wanted to find out what made a hero. We listed four heroes that we all knew, brainstormed describing words or traits for each of them, then looked to see if there were any common describing words or traits. Our heros were Ken Griffey Jr., Sheryle Swoops, Martina Hingus, and Gary Paulsen.

Results

Our group found that most of our heroes worked hard, were very good at something, and spent a lot of time practicing.

Ideas

We think an important part of being successful is working hard and practicing.

Science Skills

Many of these activities call for students to master a set of skills related to science. Important science skills include the following: observe, describe, create a diagram, create a graph, create a table, record, measure, weigh, use a data base, keep a lab notebook, predict, make groups, ask a question, create a DRC, organize data, demonstrate, conclude, write a lab report. A checklist can be created and included in a learning portfolio along with lab reports to show students' progress in learning how to "science" (see Figure 8.7).

THINKING IN SCIENCE CLASS

The thinking skills and activities described below can be incorporated into science classes to get students to think in a variety of ways.

Thinking Skills and Activities for Science

1. Fluency. Here students brainstorm to generate a list related to a particular topic. This can be done as a sponge activity, as a quick introduction to a lesson or unit, or as closure to a lesson. Students are given 15 seconds to generate as many ideas as possible. This kind of thinking improves with practice. Sometimes students enjoy competing to see who can generate the most ideas in a

Figure 8.7 Checklist for Science Skills

Science Skills

observe ___	use a data base ___
describe ___	predict ___
create a diagram ___	make groups ___
create a graph ___	ask a question ___
create a table ___	create a DRC ___
measure ___	organize data ___
record ___	demonstrate ___
use a lab report ___	conclude ___

I = introduced,   L = learned,   M = mastered

given time. You will discover interesting things about how students think which may cause you to reformulate your ideas related to intelligence.

Students might brainstorm to generate the following kinds of lists:

•Attributes of an item -- Tell as much as you can about: spinach, soil, clouds, rain, metal, rocks, rivers, fish, primates, flowers, electricity, the sun, Mexico, mountains, lakes, glaciers, winter, or leaves.

• Items that have attributes -- Name things that: have four feet, two feet, tails, bills, teeth, flat teeth, sharp teeth, hooves, long noses, beaks, feathers, lay eggs, migrate, roots, flat feet, claws, hair, scales, or gills.

• Items in a category -- Name kinds of: fish, insects, birds, reptiles, mammals, rodents, plants, flowers, trees, vegetables, types of transportation, fruits, types of energy, types of metal, round things, heavy things, or light things.

• Items that are something -- Name things that are: round, flat, hard, soft, hot, cold, rough, smooth, dangerous, high, low, underground, dirty, clean, fast, slow, complicated, simple, fat, skinny, heavy, or light.

• Items that are found someplace -- Name things found in: trees, the ground, a river, the air, cities, the country, Africa, the ocean, a lake, a forest, a school, a bus, a closet, a drawer, a garage, a car, a grocery store, a bike shop, or a classroom.

• Items that do something -- Names things that: swim, fly, hop, run fast, run slowly, crawl, dig, sing, nest, eat meat, eat grass, eat bugs, float, sink, sing, are magnetic, melt, rattle, bounce, wrinkle, snap, break, vibrate, shine, squeak, reflect, make noise, pop, burn, don't burn, shake, or pour.

• Items that contain something -- Name things that have: water, wood, heat, light, metal, glass, plastic, copper, or paper.

2. Flexibility. Given an object, concept, or item, students find new or unusual ways for it to be used or applied. Example: Give students one of the following objects and have them find a variety of alternative ways for it to be used: a hanger, fork, cup, pliers, golf tee, string, blanket, or shoe box. Example: a cup can be used for drinking, holding pennies, a hat for a monkey, a nose protector, and house for ants, a swimming pool for crickets, etc.

A game using this thinking skill is called Last Person Standing. Here, a small group is given an object. The first player holds the object and names a possible use. The object is passed and the next player must name another possible use. Players are given 10 seconds to think of a possible use before they are asked to sit down. Encourage creative and inventive thinking. The last person standing is the winner.

3. Creative Problem Solving. This thinking skill effectively complements a unit on inventors or inventions. Students begin by brainstorming different problems found in their daily lives. In small groups or individually, students design a product or invention to solve that problem. Reinforce unique and creative ideas. Products and designs can be displayed at a science or inventors' fair.

4. Generate Relationships. Look at a plant, animals, or mineral. Generate a list of attributes. Find another item that shares many of these attributes and describe the relationship. Example: A duck has feathers, webbed feet, a flat bill, walks slow, swims, and lays eggs. A beaver has webbed feet and swims. These are both animals that are found in the woods, live around water, and live in Minnesota.

5. Compare and Contrast. Compare and contrast different types of plants, rocks, soil, species, animals, or experiments. Have students use a Web-of-Comparison to organize their thinking.

6. Inferring. Bring in an item or part of an item that students may not recognize. Have students generate a list of things they know about the object and try to guess what it is or how it is used. For example, show the class the air filter from an old lawn mower. Students generate a list of things they know or can observe: It is light, spongy, smells like gas, feels greasy, etc. In small groups they ask yes or no questions until one group guesses exactly what it is or how it is used.

7. Ordering. Given a list of items or substances, students rank them from heaviest to lightest, best floater to worst floater, strongest to weakest, hardest to softest, or stickiest to least sticky, etc.

SUMMARY

1. Science is a verb -- a process of looking at and organizing the world.
2. Knowledge is an important part of the scientific process.
3. Scientists are people who ask questions and find answers.
4. Inquiry is when scientific methods are applied to a learning situation.
5. Three thinking skills reflect methods of science: creating groups, investigation, and experimenting.
6. Inquiry contains three elements: knowledge, structure, and freedom.
7. The steps of the inquiry are to ask a question, gather data, organize data, and communicate ideas about data.

References

Armbruster, B. (1993). Science and reading. <u>The Reading Teacher, 46</u>, 346-347.

Gallagher, J.J., & Gallagher, S.A. (1994). <u>Teaching the gifted child</u>. Needham Heights, MA: Allyn and Bacon.

Hodson, D. (1988). Toward a philosophically more valid science curriculum. <u>Science Education, 72,</u> 19-40.

Savage, T., & Armstrong, D. (1996). <u>Effective teaching in elementary social studies</u> (3rd ed.). Englewoods Cliffs, NJ: Prentice Hall.

Thelen, J.N. (1984). <u>Improving reading in science</u> (2nd ed.). Newark, Delaware: International Reading Association.

9

Thinking Skills and Social Studies

Students don't become life-long, self-motivated learners by listening to civics lectures for twelve years. They do it by regularly practicing the kind of inquiry, evaluations, decision-making, and action they'll be called upon to exercise later (Zemelman, Daniels, & Hyde, 1993, p. 121).

This chapter examines five areas related to thinking skills and social studies: (a) the social studies curriculum, (b) learning about self and others, (c) values, (d) newspapers and current events, and (e) inquiry.

THE SOCIAL STUDIES CURRICULUM

Social studies is the study of people and societies. It might include subjects such as history, anthropology, government or civics, economics, geography, psychology, sociology, civics, or economics. It might also include cultures, ethnicity, gender issues, interpersonal skills, values, and religions. Unfortunately, students sometimes associate social studies with learning dates, states, capitals, countries, land forms, and moralistic tips related to citizenship and American government, thus making this subject seem more mundane than exciting. So, how can social studies be made more interesting and relevant to students' lives? This is not an easy problem to solve. Too often the solution is, "Let's order a new textbook." In this chapter I am suggesting that schools redefine the problem and include thinking skills as part of the answer.

Human Class

Traditionally, social studies has used a spiral or a widening horizons approach to curriculum which starts with the child and expands outwards as it moves up in grades (Eagan, 1982). The typical spiral curriculum would look something like this:

grade one -- the child or self
grade two -- home and family
grade three -- school and local community
grade four -- the state
grade five -- the nation
grade six -- the western hemisphere and the world

However, the Bradly Commission (1988) suggested that this approach to social studies was too restrictive. I would add to this boring and irrelevant. I recommend that social studies curriculums be restructured and redefined. Instead of social studies, it ought to be thought of as human class, the goal of which would be to teach students how to be humans existing in a family, a social structure, and a world. With an increasing number of changes occurring at all levels of our society, there is a greater need than ever for classes that teach students how to be human beings.

LEARNING ABOUT SELF AND OTHERS

A major goal of human class would be to help students learn about themselves and others. Examples of possible topics might include the following:

1. Humans have thoughts and feelings.
2. Humans grow and change.
3. Humans have intellect, emotion, and spirituality.
4. Humans need to be good to themselves.
5. Humans need to be good to family and friends if they are to have them.
6. How to make good choices.
7. How to work in a group.
8. How to resolve conflicts.
9. How to work within a social group and society.
10. How groups can get along.
11. How to be good to our planet.
12. Interesting and important human beings.
13. How all humans are the same.
14. How humans are different.
15. How humans govern themselves.
16. Where humans live.
17. How humans attain wants and needs.
18. What humans have done along the way (history).

Thinking Skills and Activities for Learning About Self and Others

An integral component of human class will be to learn about self and others. The following thinking skills and activities can be used to this end.

1. Brainstorm. Students brainstorm attributes that describe them, then put them into groups to answer the question, "Who are you?" To extend this, students arrange these attributes in order from most important to least important, or those liked best to those liked least.

2. Web and Brainstorm. Students think of three important people in their lives. They create a web with themselves in the center and the three important people listed as the nodes along the outside (see Figure 9.1). Then, they brainstorm attributes or experiences had with each. Students can also use this skill to examine and describe important events, places, or things in their lives.

Figure 9.1 Web and Brainstorm – Important People

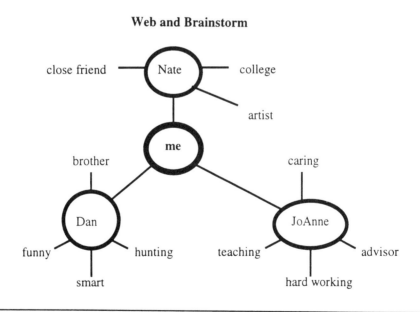

Web and Brainstorm

3. Compare. Organize students into small groups to generate words and phrases that describe each member. Students then use the Compare-O-Graph (Figure 9.2) to gather and organize this information and to look for commonalities. Finally, each group describes itself in terms of the similarities. To extend this activity, students can compare themselves to characters found in history, literature, or current events.

Figure 9.2 Compare-O-Graph Used to Find Commonalities

Compare-O-Graph

descriptors	Billy	JoAnne	Susan

4. *Compare and Contrast.* This activity works well as an introductory activity at beginning of the year. Students find another person in the room and use the Web-of-Comparison to discover at four least similarities and differences. Students can also compare and contrast things such as traits, values, views, strengths, and weaknesses.

5. *Creating Groups.* Students quickly brainstorm events that have happened to them during the week. These events are then arranged into groups and reported in terms of their groups (these data can be graphed and comparisons can be made). This activity can be extended by examining national or community events, or by having students look at events that have happened to them during the year or throughout their life.

6. *Investigation.* This is an inquiry activity where students gather data, put data into groups in order to understand them and describe them to others. Students are given a question, such as, "What makes a good friend?" Working in small groups they put this question to 20-30 different people and record their response. After all the answers are collected, students look for types of responses, designate categories, and move the responses into categories. Results are reported in terms of the groups and numbers of responses found in each group (these data can also be graphed). Other types of questions might include: What activities do students do on the playground? What are the second grade's favorite kind of dessert? What is your favorite outdoor activity? A list of inquiry questions to use for social studies is in the Inquiry section on page 114.

7. *Ordering.* Here, students brainstorm to generate at least 10 items or events in their lives. Then, they put them in order according to a given criterion. For example, events can be arranged from most recent to least recent, most important to least important, biggest to smallest, hardest to easiest, hardest to

softest, most helpful to least helpful, happiest to saddest, or most fun to most boring.

This can be extended by having students create a line graph. Their life events are listed chronologically along the horizontal axis; along the vertical axis students rate their lives according to the given criteria (see Figure 9.3).

Figure 9.3 Line Graph Used to List and Rate Life Events

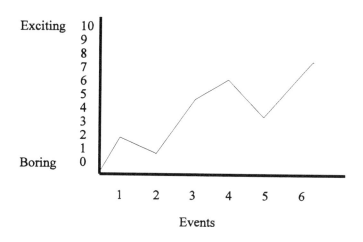

1. High school choir concert.
2. High school graduation.
3. First year of college.
4. College homecoming.
5. College graduation.
6. First year of teaching.

8. Investigation. In a large group, students generate a list of activities they have engaged in during the last week. Students then put them in order from most important to least important in their journals. An inquiry activity can be designed here by asking one of the following questions: "Are there common activities that are preferred by all students? Does this preference change as students grow older? Do females have different activity preferences than males?"

9. Flexibility. Examine a problem that students have at home or at school. In small groups, students brainstorm to generate ways to solve that problem.

Encourage a wide variety of ideas, making sure to recognize practical as well as highly creative and unusual solutions.

10. Evaluation/Critique. In large group or small groups, students define four traits of a particular kind of person. For example: What are four traits of a good friend, hero, villain, leader, hunter, politician, actor, or business person? These traits are used as criteria to rate or rank people from history, literature, or current events. Example: Heroes are brave, kind, smart, and action-oriented. Four heroes found in literature and real life are Michael Jordan, Dorothy Gale from the <u>Wizard of Oz</u>, Luke Skywalker, and Abraham Lincoln. A DRC chart is then used to rank each of these heroes on the four traits listed (see Figure 9.4).

Figure 9.4 Using a Compare-O-Graph to Rank Heroes

Ranking Heros

Heros	brave	kind	smart	action-oriented	Total
Michael Jordan	2	1	2	3	8
Dorothy from Oz	1	4	1	2	8
Luke Skywalker	4	2	3	4	13
Abraham Lincoln	3	3	4	1	11

Heroes ranked from highest to lowest: 4 = highest, 1 = lowest.

TEACHING VALUES

A value is a trait or quality that one finds important. Values are different than morality. Morality is a code of behavior based on a value. Just as each individual has different values, so there are many different concepts of moral behavior. It is possible, however, to find values with which most would agree and teach them (Ellis, 1998). These values might include traits such as honesty, creativity, loyalty, hard work, cooperation, participation, self-discipline, responsibility, dignity, freedom, positive attitude, equality of all, compassion, or kindness. These are values which can be taught explicitly without alienating most groups within a community.

In examining these values teachers cannot assume that students have full knowledge of these words or concepts; therefore, teaching values should begin with a definition and direct instruction (Ellis, 1998). Figure 9.5 shows an example of a values lesson with direct instruction and a thinking skill used to create an activity.

Figure 9.5 Values lesson -- Compassion

Grade 5

OBJECTIVE: Students will learn about compassion.
INTRO: A value is a trait or characteristic that a person thinks is important. Compassion is one value that many people think is important.
INPUT:
1. Compassion means caring and wanting to help people in need.
2. Compassionate people notice people who need help.
A. They feel sorry for them.
B. They want to help them.
3. Compassionate people understand and care for others.
A. They care for the feelings of others.
B. They care for the health and safety of others.
4. Compassionate people will not tease or make others feel bad.
5. Compassionate people try to understand others.
A. They are friendly.
B. They like all kinds of people.
C. They have lots of friends.
6. Compassionate people make good doctors, teachers, and friends.
ACTIVITY:
   Small Group Activity
1. In our story _Bridge to Teribithia_ (Pattersen, 1977), we've encountered several characters so far.
A. Jess, Leslie, May Belle, Miss Edmunds, Mrs. Myers.
2. In your group, rank them from most compassionate to least.
A. Be prepared to describe your most and least compassionate person.
B. Tell why you picked them as such.
   Individual Activity
1. In your journal, write the statement, Jess Aaron is a compassionate person.
2. Gather information to support that statement.
3. Describe a real life person that you think is compassionate.

Thinking Skills and Activities for Teaching Values

After some direct instruction, the following thinking skills and activities will help students begin to form or come to conclusions about their own values.

1. Fluency. Students brainstorm to find different examples of a particular value found in real life, literature, history, or current events. Example: Self-discipline is a value. Help students generate examples and instances in music, sports, science, or the arts where people have demonstrated this value in order to succeed.

2. Flexibility. Using an action from literature, history, current events, or students' lives, students find alternative actions which demonstrate a particular value. For example, in the story *The Three Little Pigs*, what might have happened if all three of the pigs had all cooperated in building their houses?

3. Originality. Students create an advertising campaign along with brochures, posters, or TV commercials to promote a particular value.

4. Compare. Students find a group of people who embody a particular value, then use a Compare-O-Graph to find life events or traits they have in common (see Figure 9.6). These people can be selected from students' lives, literature, history, or current events.

Figure 9.6 Compare-O-Graph for Looking at Common Traits

Compare-O-Graph

	Katherine Pattersen	Jess Aarons	Robin Williams
creativity			

5. Compare and Contrast. Students select two people who embody a particular value or who represent opposite ends of a value spectrum. Then they use a Web-of-Comparison to examine the similarities and differences in life events or traits. For example, while studying compassion, Mother Teresa might be compared with Joan Collins, Francis of Assisi with Christopher Columbus, or

Jess Aarons to Gilly Hopkins.

   6. Supporting a Statement. Here, the teacher or students make a particular value statement regarding a famous person found in current events, literature, or history. Then, students then find clues or information to support the statement. A data retrieval chart can be used to guide this process (see Figure 9.7). When examining more than one person, a Compare-O-Graph can be used to gather and organize information (see Figure 9.8).

   7. Ordering. Given a value, students rank a series of actions, events, or a group of famous people using that value as a criterion. These can be selected from literature, history, or current events. Ordered lists can then be recorded on posters, bulletin boards, or in learning logs or journals.

   To extend this, students are given a list of values and asked to rank them from most important to least important in their journals. An inquiry activity can be designed here by asking one of the following questions: "Are there some values which seem to be most preferred and least preferred? Do these values change as students grow older? Do adults have different values than children? Do females have different values than males?"

Figure 9.7 A DRC for Supporting a Statement

Support a Statement

Statement	Supporting Information
Martin Luther King Jr. was brave.	

Figure 9.8 A Compare-O-Graph for Supporting a Statement

Compare-O-Graph

People

Trait	Black Elk	Rosa Parks	Martin Luther King Jr.
Bravery			

---

8. Decision Making. This is sometimes referred to as values clarification, moral dilemmas, or moral decision-making. Here, students work in small groups to examine a situation or a problem in which a decision must be made. A list of possible solutions is generated along with the positive and negative consequences of that solution. Students come to a consensus as to the best action, and list at least three reasons to support their decision. One of the advantages of this technique is that students are exposed to multiple perspectives and the reasoning of others. This helps them move more readily from one moral reasoning stage to another. A DRC is helpful here in gathering and organizing ideas (see Figure 9.9).

9. Discussion Web. This is a form of *Decision Making* adapted from an idea by Donna Alvermann (1991). In traditional classroom discussions, there is always the danger that the teacher and a few highly verbal students will monopolize the talk. The discussion web provides an opportunity for all students to express their ideas. It also promotes discussion and allows for multiple viewpoints to be expressed. With adaptation, it can be used in kindergarten through high school.

Figure 9.9 DRC for Decision Making

Decision Making

Problem:

Solution	Positive Consequences	Negative Consequences

Decision:

Supporting Statements:

Steps

1. After reading a story, chapter, article, or discussing an event, the teacher finds a question that has a yes - no answer.
2. A pair of students are given one web and asked to find ideas that support each side of the question (see Figure 9.10).
3. The pair mixes with another pair to form a small-group. The small-group compares webs, and adds new ideas on both sides of the question to create a new web. The goal of this small-group is to reach consensus. All members may not necessarily agree with their group's answer, but they will get a chance to describe their ideas later during class discussion or in their journals.

Figure 9.10 Discussion Web

Discussion Web

Yes   *No*

Question

4. One speaker from each small-group shares his or her group's conclusion. The speaker has two minutes to share and must give at least three reasons to support the group's conclusion.
5. Individuals describe their opinions in their learning logs.
6. The issue is opened for class discussion.

Adaptations for Younger Students
1. With kindergarten and first grade students, the discussion web is used only in large group. Here, the teacher records all of the students' ideas on a large chart or the front board.
2. Steps 3 and 4 above are skipped.

NEWSPAPERS AND CURRENT EVENTS

Using newspapers and current events helps students connect school life to life outside the classroom. One goal of social studies is to develop citizens who can critically analyze the issues and events happening around them to make good decisions.

Thinking Skills and Activities for Newspapers and Current Events

1. Elaboration. There are two ways this thinking skill can be used with newspapers. First, students find a product in an ad and look for ways to improve the product or the ad better. Or, the teacher pulls sentences or paragraphs from the newspaper and students find ways to make them more interesting.

2. Flexibility. Using a sentence or paragraph in the newspaper, students generate as many ways to express the same idea as they can.

3. Originality. Students find a product from a newspaper ad and design their own video commercials, signs, or newspaper ad.

4. Integrate. Using newspaper ads for different products, students combine them to come up with a brand new product or device. Then, they create a newspaper ad for their new product.

5. Creating Groups. Students record newspaper headlines over a period of time and put them into groups. The types of groups and frequency of items in each group are reported. This data can be graphed and comparison can be made with other newspapers, types of publications, or time periods.

6. Ordering. Headlines are ordered according to a given criteria: most important to least, happiest to saddest, etc. To extend this, a line graph is created. Headlines are listed chronologically along the horizontal axis and rated according to a given criterion along the vertical axis (see example in Figure 9.3).

7. Compare and Contrast. Students compare a 200-word section of a headline story to a 200-word section of a sports story. What is similar? Different? This can be extended by comparing and contrasting this section to a section from a textbook and a narrative book or by comparing one newspaper to another.

8. Analysis. Students examine the newspaper to determine one or all of the following: What goes into a newspaper? What makes up a sports section? What comprises a news section, want ads, entertainment section, etc.?

9. Investigation. Students examine a 100-word section of newspaper text. An inquiry is designed by asking one of the following question: What is this section comprised of? How many sentences? Adjectives? How many adjectives per sentence (APS)? What is the average length of each sentence? This data can be graphed and comparisons can be made to other types of text.

10. Investigation. What makes a good comic strip? Students design a survey to answer this question. Do females like different comic strips than males? Do younger children like different comic strips than older children?

11. Observe and Conclude. Students select an editorial and use a DRC (Figure 9.11) to list the facts and opinions. These data are used to come to their own conclusion.

12. Inference. Students select an editorial and use the Infer-O-Gram to make inferences about the author. The inference question might be: How might we describe the writer of this editorial? Who is this author? What kind of person is this author? What political party does this author belong to?

Figure 9.11 DRC for Sorting Facts and Opinions

Facts and Opinions

Issue:

Facts	Opinions

Conclusion:

---

13. Support a Statement. After reading a news story, the student or teacher makes a statement relative to that story. Students then find and list details from the news story to support that statement (use DRC Figure 9.7).

14. Creative Problem Solving. Students identify a problem found in the newspaper (problems might also be taken from the school, community, or classroom). In small groups, students generate solutions, pick the best solution, refine and embellish it, then present their solutions to the class. Examples of problems: How can we reduce crime in our neighborhood? How can we prevent teenage smoking? How can we make the lunch line go faster? How can we solve the fighting that is happening on the playground? How can we come to consensus on an issue?

15. Critique/Evaluation. Students define the criteria for a good movie. (This naturally leads to discussions about movie genre.) Then, newspaper ads are found for movies students have seen. Students rate these movies on their criteria (see Figure 9.12). This can be extended by looking at several movies and ranking them according to a criterion (Figure 9.13).

Figure 9.12 DRC for a Movie Critique -- Rating

Rating Movies

Movie: <u>The Wizard of Oz</u>

Criteria	Rating
Has a good plot or story.	3
Has plenty of action.	4
Has interesting lead characters.	4
Has a happy ending.	3

Total: 14

Rating: 4 = very high, 3 = good, 2 = average, 1 = low

Figure 9.13 DRC for Movie Critique -- Ranking

Ranking Movies

Criteria

Movie	1	2	3	4	Total
The Wizard of Oz	2	2	2	4	10
Jurassic Park	3	4	1	1	9
Star Wars	4	3	3	2	12
ET	1	1	4	3	9

Ranking: 4 = highest; 1 = lowest

Criteria
1. Has a good plot or story.
2. Has plenty of action.
3. Has interesting lead characters.
4. Has a happy ending.

16. Decision Making. This is a small group activity where students are presented with a problem taken from the newspaper or one that is present in the school or the community. In large-group, solutions are generated. Each group then picks the top five and lists them on the DRC (see Figure 9.14). Each student within that group ranks the solutions from highest to lowest. The total ranking score for each solution is tallied and a decision is made based on that score.

Figure 9.14 DRC for Decision Making by Ranking

Ranking Solutions to Problems

Each group member ranks the solutions 1-5, with 5 being the highest and 1 being the lowest ranking. Totals for all students' rankings are tabulated in the far right column.

Problem: Local businesses need to attract more customers.

Solutions	Jim	Mary	Sue	Pat	TOTAL
Put up more signs around town.	4	1	2	5	12
Lower prices.	1	5	1	4	11
Build restaurants, movie theaters, and entertainment venues.	2	4	4	3	13
Change the types of items sold.	3	3	3	2	11
Use more advertising in newspapers and television.	5	2	2	1	10

Decision: Local business owners should try to encourage the development of restaurants, movies theaters, miniature golf, video arcades, and things that people would come to for entertainment. This would increase the number of visitors and amount of business.

INQUIRY IN SOCIAL STUDIES

The previous chapter described inquiry and showed how to design inquiry activities. Listed here are 90 inquiry questions which might be used with a social studies or human class unit at various grade levels. Students should be encouraged to use interviews or other primary data sources to answer the questions. Most of these questions will need some type of DRC to help students collect and organize data. Data can be described using tables, charts, bar graphs, pict-o-graphs, line graphs, diagrams, or time line and presented using some form of a lab report.

Possible Inquiry Questions for Human Class

1. What color socks did students wear today?
2. What kind of weather is it today?
3. What do we like to eat for dessert?
4. What size are our families?
5. What are things we like to do with our families?
6. What kinds of jobs do our parents have?
7. What kinds of pets do we have?
8. What is our favorite kind of garden food?
9. What is our favorite fruit?
10. Where do we buy our groceries?
11. What are our favorite TV shows?
12. Where does catsup come from?
13. Where does our water come from?
14. How many police officers are in our town?
15. What does a police officer do?
16. What does a fire fighter do?
17. Where do we live?
18. What kind of job might we want when we get older? (Here, students collect data related to training, job prospects, and salary.)
19. What is our heritage?
20. What makes a good friend?
21. What was it like growing up in the 40's, 50's, or 60's?
22. What do people remember about the Vietnam war?
23. What do people remember about the Korean war?
24. What do people remember about World War II?
25. Where is a good place to take a vacation?
26. What was Lincoln's childhood like?
27. What made Lincoln a good president?
28. What made Martin Luther King Jr. a great leader?
29. What is a good leader?
30. What is a compassionate person?
31. What traits are important in getting a job?
32. What is a good citizen?
33. What are the most important events that have happened in the last week?

Month? Year? Decade? Century? Millennium?

34. What are the most important events of 1976?
35. Where and when did <u>The Bridge to Teribithia</u> (Pattersen, 1973) take place?
36. What is a democracy?
37. What makes a good government?
38. How do people solve differences in families, classrooms, schools, communities, or countries.
39. What makes a good president?
40. What is the purpose of religion in our society?
41. What laws help keep us safe?
42. What are the important laws in our community, state, or country?
43. What are the important rules we have in our classroom, school, or family?
44. What kinds of jobs do our parents have?
45. What laws help protect our environment?
46. How do we get rid of wastes?
47. How much garbage does our family throw out each day/week?
48. What people have made a positive difference in our school, community, state, or country?
49. What is a hero?
50. Who are our heroes?
51. What values do we feel are important?
52. What kinds of problems do families sometimes face?
53. What kinds of problems are found in our classroom, school, community, state, or nation?
54. What should you do if somebody teases you?
55. How can you make somebody feel good?
56. How is your life different than that of somebody living in Japan, Russia, or South Africa?
57. How is your school different today than it was 10, 20, 40, or 100 years ago?
58. What inventions have changed our world?
59. What inventions have changed music?
60. What kind of music does our class, school, community prefer?
61. Do girls like different kinds of music than boys?
62. Do older students like different kinds of music than younger students?
63. What kind of music do adults like? Older adults? Younger adults?
64. Where do most people get their news?
65. What are the wants and needs of people in our school, class, or community?
66. What does our class, school, or community like to do in their leisure time?
67. Where do we get our food?
68. How has transportation changed in the last 5, 10, 20, 50, and 100 years?

69. What products do we export? Import?
70. What important services are found in our community?
71. How far do students live from school?
72. How do students get to school?
73. What lakes, rivers, mountains, deserts are found in our community, state, county, state, country, or hemisphere?
74. How many community members or parents were in the services?
75. What kinds of energy do we use each day?
76. What energy source is used to heat/cool our homes?
77. Where does our energy come from?
78. How is a desert different from a forest?
79. How did western pioneers get their food?
80. What were the most important inventions developed during the industrial revolution?
81. How have airplanes changed the way people live?
82. What Native American tribes lived in our region in the last 200 years? What happened to them?
83. What are the most important inventions of the last 5, 10, 50, 100, or 1000 years?
84. What was life like as a slave in 1800?
85. What problems did early settlers face?
86. What problems did Native Americans face before settlers came? After settlers came?
87. How did Christianity, Islam, Judaism, Buddhism, and Hinduism originate?
88. What are the similarities between the five major religions?
89. How do different countries protect religious freedom?

SUMMARY

1. Social studies is the study of people and societies.
2. A good social studies curriculum teaches students how to exist in a family, social structure, and the world.
3. Thinking skills and social studies can be used to help students explore intrapersonal dimensions.
4. Thinking skills and social studies can be used to help students examine and clarify values.
5. Newspapers and current events provide a rich source for thinking skills and social studies activities.
6. Inquiry can be used to enhance social studies.

References

Alvermann, D. (1991). The discussion web: A graphic aid for learning across the curriculum. The Reading Teacher, 45, 92-98.

Bradley Commission on History in Schools. (1988). Building a history curriculum: Guidelines for teaching history in schools. Washington CED: Educational Excellence Network.

Eagan, K. (1982). Teaching history to young people. Phi Delta Kappan, 64, 439-441.

Ellis, A. (1998). Teaching and learning elementary social studies (6th ed.). Needham Heights, MA: Allyn and Bacon.

Pattersen, K. (1977). A Bridge to Teribithia. New York: HarperCollins.

10

Thinking Skills and the Gifted

This chapter outlines ways in which thinking skills can be used to meet the needs of the gifted within the classroom.

GIFTEDNESS

Amy was a very talented long distance runner. When she began her first season as a high school freshmen, her times were much faster than anyone else's on the track team. However, in practice, all distance runners were given the same training routine. All ran the same distances each day and did the same number of sprints and other exercises. Still, Amy won all the distance events in local track meets. At the end of the season, she placed first in the regional meet which qualified her to advance to the state track meet. Here, for the first time, she faced runners of equal ability. Sadly, Amy placed well out of first place. She, like many of the gifted students in our classrooms, never reached her full potential because she was offered the same training routine as everyone else. But, same does not mean equal. We recognize this in our athletes; yet with our learners we continue to offer the same academic training routine to all students regardless of their ability or unique needs. Why is this?

Squeamishness

Schools are often squeamish about recognizing intellectually or creatively gifted students. Why is this? It may be that many still do not understand the nature of intelligence. They cling to the old notion that intelligence is a single, fixed entity, and those with higher scores are destined for lives of privilege while those with lower scores, lives of servitude. This leads to a misplaced and groundless fear of elitism and snobbishness (which, by the way, seems to be accepted in athletes but not in thinkers.)

What Giftedness Might Be

There can be no denying that there are students in every classroom who think in ways which allow them to flourish in certain environments and to create outstanding products or performances. These are the gifted students who have learning needs related to their unique form of speciality. The Department of Education defines gifted students as:

> *Children and youth with outstanding talent perform or show the potential for performing at remarkably high levels of accomplishment when compared with others of their age, experience, or environment. They exhibit high performance capability in intellectually, creative and/or artistic areas, possess an unusual leadership capacity, or excel in specific academic fields. They require services or activities not ordinarily provided by the schools (National Excellence, pp. 54-55, 1993).*

Renzulli and Reis (1997) offer a definition of giftedness which is more inclusive and focuses on behaviors:

> *Gifted behaviors reflects ... an interaction among three basic clusters of human traits -- these clusters being above average (but not necessarily high) general and/or specific ability, high levels of task commitment (motivation), and high levels of creativity. Gifted and talented children are those possessing or capable of developing this composite set of traits and applying them to any potentially valuable area of human behavior.*

Both of these definitions take into account the notion of multiple ways of demonstrating giftedness and thus complement the descriptions of creativity and intelligence found in Chapters 4 and 5 of this text.

PROGRAMMING OPTIONS

Described below are ways in which the curriculum might be differentiated to meet the special needs of creative and intellectually gifted learners within their regular classrooms. Keep in mind, however, that good education for the gifted is good education for all. Those techniques and strategies used to meet the needs of gifted learners will enhance the curriculum of all learners. The difference is not in the quality but in quantity. Whereas all children benefit from open-ended activities and creative projects which require the use of thinking skills, gifted learners need these in greater degree.

Ineffective Programming Options for Gifted Learners

1. MOTS (more of the same). Using this strategy, students who finish their work early are given more work to do. This option should be avoided. When accomplishment is rewarded with more work, students soon learn to mask their talents.

2. Grouping for Acceleration. Here, students are grouped, usually in math or reading, so they can move through a curriculum at a faster pace. However, the benefits are slight when each group is given the same curriculum (Kulik, 1992). That is, gifted learners are given the same curriculum only faster.

3. Tracking. Students who are tracked are put into homogeneous groups for all classes based on a test or past achievement. Tracking is not the same as ability grouping (Feldhusen & Moon, 1992; Fielder, Lange, & Winebrenner, 1993). In tracking, one score determines which group students are in for all subject areas. They rarely move from one group to another. Ability grouping is flexible and is used for one subject, usually math and reading. In the past, tracking was used primarily in middle schools and high schools. This strategy is rarely used today.

4. Cooperative Learning. While this is an effective learning tool in the classroom, there is no valid research to support its use as a strategy for meeting the needs of gifted learners (Feldhusen & Moon, 1992; Fiedler et al., 1993). With cooperative learning groups, gifted learners are often put in the role of teacher or tutor, or end up doing most of the work (Davis & Rimm, 1998). This adds more stress and inhibits rather than promotes growth.

5. Work Done in Isolation. Students are sent off to the library to read a book or off to a computer to work by themselves. While this may seem appropriate initially, students do not enjoy the sense of isolation. Also, it punishes the gifted learner by denying that student instruction and teacher contact. Would we do the same with our gifted athletes?

Effective Programming Options for Gifted Learners

1. Cross-Graded Classrooms. In selected subject areas, usually math or reading, high ability students are put with students at a higher grade level. For example, a second grade student may go to a fifth grade classroom for mathematics. This allows gifted learners to interact with age-appropriate peers for the majority of the day and results in substantial gains when compared to gifted students in mixed ability classrooms (Kulik, 1992; Rodgers, 1993).

2. Compacting and Differentiation. Using this strategy, students show mastery of the basic elements of a chapter or unit during a pre-test, then pursue related research or open-ended projects designed by the teacher which call for more complex levels of thinking and the use of thinking skills. For example, in a social studies unit students would read the necessary material and demonstrate proficiency by attaining a base-level criterion score on a pre-test. Then, individuals or small groups would contract to do independent work. Students are graded, not on the pre-test, but on the independent projects. Figure 10.1 shows a form that might be used here. One of the benefits of this strategy is that formal identification is not necessary. All students have the chance to show proficiency and do special projects.

*3. Cluster Grouping Within Heterogeneous Classroom*s. At each grade level, five to eight gifted learners are placed in the classroom of a teacher trained in the use of thinking skills and classroom strategies for gifted learners (Fielder et al., 1993). This allows gifted learners to have access to like-minded peers as well as a curriculum which is differentiated to meet their needs and is a very effective use of limited educational resources.

4. Embedded Thinking Skills. Thinking skills are embedded into a curriculum to produce open-ended activities and assignments which value student ideas and ways of thinking. Also, by assigning a number to each thinking skill, it is easy to document what thinking skills were used in various subject areas in a weekly planner. Thus, when a parent or curriculum examiner asks how the needs of the gifted learner were being met, one can point to where thinking skills were used.

5. Ability Grouping. See below.

Ability Grouping

Because of the amount of confusion and misinformation related to this subject, this programming option is described separately. With this strategy students are grouped within or between classes according to their ability in a particular subject area. This is usually done with math and reading and is *much different than tracking.*

Students at different levels have different needs (Felhusen & Moon, 1992). Low achieving students need more scaffolded learning experiences while high achieving students need to move more quickly through skills instruction and examine concepts in greater depth. Putting students into flexible groups within a classroom or between classrooms is and designing the curriculum to meet the particular needs of the group is an effective programming option *for students at all ability levels* (Feldhusen & Moon, 1992; Fiedler et al., 1993; Kulik, 1992; Rogers, 1993; Shield, 1995; Piirto, 1994). In issues of self-esteem, Kulik (1992) found that the self-esteem of low and average achieving learners actually

Figure 10.1 Independent Research

Independent Research

This research will allow you to investigate a topic that you are interested in. Don't be concerned with a particular length, depth, or breadth of your research. Instead, concentrate on finding an interesting topic and gathering supporting material. Some very good research is short and concise. The following steps should help you plan and implement your independent research:

1. Ask a question: What do you want to find out about? What are you interested in? Look for questions. Talk to people. Read magazines or books, watch TV, or check the Internet to find ideas that you think are interesting or important.

2. Gather data: Get some information about your question. Use at least two different sources. (Older students should use 4-6 different sources.) Observe, record, listen, ask questions, interview experts, survey people, read books and magazines, use the Internet.

3. Record data and look for patterns: Record the interesting or important ideas you find. Look for common themes or patterns. Organize your data into groups. Don't be afraid to throw away data that are not important.

4. Answer your questions: Answer your original question. Use the data to come up with your own ideas or answers.

5. Communicate your ideas: Present your findings to an audience. You can create a speech, demonstration, drama, report, video, drawing, sculpture, dance or creative movement, research report, or use graphs, charts, and tables.

Grading Criteria
Your independent research will be graded on the following criteria:

1. Responsibility -- Responsibility is demonstrated in the following ways: (a) the researcher was able to come up with a question or idea, (b) the research was completed in the prescribed time, and (c) the researcher gathered appropriate sources for data.

2. Knowledge -- The research (a) is interesting and informative, (b) demonstrates a knowledge base, and (c) uses an appropriate number of sources.

3. Thinking -- The research (a) finds important ideas or themes, (b) uses data to come to a conclusion or answer a question, and (c) shows the researcher as a reflective learner.

4. Communication -- The presentation (a) communicates background knowledge and new ideas effectively, (b) is free of mistakes and of professional quality, (c) is clear, logical, and organized, (d) is concise and uses academic language, and (e) is interesting.

---

increased with ability grouping. Here, instruction was comfortably paced. Instead of failing, they were succeeding. The self-esteem of high achieving learners actually decreased slightly. This is because for the first time they were with equals and did not stand out.

SUMMARY

1. Gifted learners have special learning needs that must be addressed if they are to reach their full potential.
2. Schools should recognize and reward gifted thinkers in the same way in which they do gifted athletes.
3. Giftedness is a combination of creativity, ability, and task commitment.
4. Ineffective programming options for gifted learners include: MOTS, grouping for acceleration, tracking, cooperative learning, and work done in isolation.
5. Effective programming options for gifted learners include: cross-graded classrooms, compacting and differentiation, cluster grouping, embedded thinking skills, and ability grouping.
6. Research shows ability grouping to be an effective strategy for students of all ability levels when instruction is designed to meet the needs of each group.

References

Davis, G., & Rimm, S. (1998). Education of the gifted and talented (4th ed.). Needham Heights, MA: Allyn & Bacon.

Fedlhusen, J.F., & Moon, S.M. (1992). Grouping gifted students: Issues and concerns. Gifted Child Quarterly, 36, 63-67.

Fielder, E.D., Lange, R.E., & Winebrenner, S. (1993). In search of reality: Unraveling the myths about tracking, ability grouping and the gifted. Roeper Review, 16, 4-7.

Gamoran, A., & Berends, M. (1987). The effects of stratification in secondary schools: Synthesis of survey and ethnographic research. Review of Educational Research, 57, 415-435.

Kulik, J.A., & Kulik, C.C. (1990). Ability grouping and gifted students. In N. Colangelo and G.A. Davis (Eds.), Handbook of gifted education (pp. 178-196). Boston: Allyn and Bacon.

Kulik, J.A. (1992). An analysis of the research on ability grouping: Historical and contemporary perspectives. The National Research Center on the Gifted and Talented. University of Connecticut, Storrs, CT.

National excellence: A case for developing America's talent. (1993). Washington, DC: U.S. Department of Education, Office of Educational Research and Improvement.

Piirto, J. (1994). Talented children and adults: Their development and education. New York: Macmillan.

Renzulli, J., & Reis, S. The schoolwide enrichment model: New directions for developing high-end learning. In N. Colangelo & G.A. Davis (Eds.), Handbook of gifted education (2nd ed.), (pp. 136-154). Boston, MA: Allyn & Bacon.

Rodgers, K.B. (1993). Grouping the gifted and talented: Questions and answers. Roper Review, 16, 8-12.

Shields, C. (1995). A comparison study of student attitudes and perceptions in homogeneous and heterogeneous classrooms. Roeper Review, 17, 234-238.

11

Thinking Skills, Standards, and Assessment

The latest trend in education is a move towards standards based education. This chapter examines (a) standardized tests and (b) performance based standards.

INCREASING SCORES ON STANDARDIZED TESTS

It is very easy to make scores go up on standardized tests. Simply spend an hour a day practicing test-taking strategies using sample questions which are similar to those found on standardized tests. These could be taught using the thinking frames below.

Thinking Frames for Standardized Tests

1. Answering Story Problems: Students will read a story problem and select the best of several responses.
Thinking Frame
A. Read the problem and question.
B. Look at all the answers.
C. Eliminate those that do not fit.
D. Find one that seems right.
E. Re-read and check.

2. Answering Math Problems: Students will read a math problem and select the best of several responses (always use scratch paper).
Thinking Frame
A. Read the problem.
B. Record the important numbers.
C. Decide on the operation.
D. Plug in the numbers and work.
E. Re-read and check to see if it makes sense.

If this were done each day of the school year, test scores would indeed go up (along with boredom and hostility), but real learning would go down as students are deprived of the joy of discovery and self-expression. It is prudent, however, to implement some sort of daily test-taking instruction before standardized testing occurs. This instruction should be relatively short and begin no sooner than two weeks before testing.

PERFORMANCE BASED STANDARDS

Performances based standards define a set of skills to be mastered (Noddings, 1997). These tasks should be specific enough to be measured, yet flexible enough to be used in a variety of academic situations (Reigeluth, 1997). In Minnesota, school districts are required to use a set of state-mandated performance based standards to create performance packages. Performance packages are a series of tasks that students must perform to demonstrate their level of mastery on each skill.

Meeting Individual Standards

Below, are some of Minnesota's performance based standards and examples of how thinking skills can be used to teach and assess them. Each of the products created would be placed in students' portfolios to demonstrate mastery of the skill.

Standards
1. Students will be able to read, view, and listen to non-fiction and fiction selections to identify main ideas and supporting details. The thinking skill *Web and Brainstorm* can be used here. After reading a story or chapter, students create a web with supporting nodes (bubbles) and brainstorm on each.
2. Students will be able to retell main events or ideas in sequence. The thinking skill, *Ordering* can be used here. After reading a story or chapter, students brainstorm those events they thought were most interesting or important. Using time as the criteria, students arrange them in order. For an expository chapter, students list interesting or important ideas. These can be arranged according to most to least interesting, most to least important, or most to least familiar.
3. Students will be able to make predictions based on information in the selection. Similar to *Inferring*, the process of *Predicting* can be broken into parts and explicitly taught. A Predict-O-Gram (Figure 11.1) can be used here.

Thinking Frame

A. Identify what is known (text clues).

B. Identify other information (other important knowledge you might have).

C. Decide what might happen next based on A and B.

Figure 11.1 Predict-O-Gram

Predict-O-Gram

Text Clues	Knowledge Clues

Prediction:

---

4. Students will be able to compare and contrast settings, ideas, or actions. The thinking skill *Compare and Contrast* would be used here. Students would compare any of the above elements using a Web-of-Comparison.

5. Students will understand ideas not stated explicitly in the selection. The thinking skill *Inferring* would be used here. An Infer-O-Gram can be used here.

Checklist

Along with the sample products above, a checklist can be used to check off each skill (Figure 11.2). Here, the students and the teacher would rate the success of each skill. This allows students to be a part of the assessment process. This also would be included in students' portfolios.

Figure 11.2 Checklist to Assess Individual Skills

Checklist of Skills

4 = outstanding, 3 = very good, 2 = average, 1 = low

Student	Skill	Teacher
	Web and Brainstorm	
	Ordering	
	Predict-O-Gram	
	Web-of-Comparison	
	Predict-O-Gram	

Student _____

Teacher _____

Grade _____

Comments:

Meeting Multiple Standards

Below is an example of how one inquiry task can be used to meet multiple performance standards. Each of the three tasks described here uses thinking skills in some form. It is assumed that before these tasks were attempted, students would have received instruction in each of their elements.

Standards

1. Reading. The student will be able to read and apply technical instructions to perform an action (reading).

2. Writing and speaking. The student will be able to prepare and give a demonstration to an audience which includes (a) describing a step-by-step procedure to complete an action, (b) using visuals or manipulatives to illustrate ideas, (c) demonstrating effective delivery techniques, and (d) answering questions from the audience concerning the demonstration.

3. Math -- chance and data handling. The student will be able to answer questions by (a) collecting and organizing data, (b) representing data using graphs and charts, and (c) communicating the results.

4. Math -- chance and data handling. The student will be able to (a) conduct experiments involving uncertainty; (b) tally, record, and explain results; and (c) use the results to predict future outcomes.

5. Math -- chance and data handling. The student will be able to represent data using at least two graphic forms.

6. Inquiry -- observation and investigation. The student will be able to answer a question by gathering data from (a) direct observations or experiments with a variable, including framing a question; (b) collecting, recording, and displaying data; (c) identifying patterns, comparing individual findings to large group findings; and (d) identifying areas for further investigation.

7. Inquiry -- observation and investigation. The student will be able to answer a question by gathering data from direct observation and interviews which include (a) identifying a topic or area for investigation, (b) writing a detailed description of the observation, (c) conducting an interview with follow-up questions, (d) designing or conducting a survey, (e) recording and organizing information, and (f) evaluating the findings in order to identify areas for further investigation.

8. Scientific methods. Students will be able to make systematic observations of objects, events, or phenomena by recording data and predicting change.

Task #1: The Reading Inquiry

Directions: Read a trade book of your choice. After finishing, follow the directions below.
1. List the 12 events you think are most interesting or important.
2. Put them into groups.
3. Create a graph to show your groups.
4. Create a lab report to communicate your findings.
5. Share your findings with the class.
   To extend:
1. Compare and contrast to another story you have read.
2. Use the same categories.
3. Create a graph to show your comparison.

Task #2: The Movie Inquiry

Directions: What kinds of movies do students in your grade prefer? Do girls like different kinds of movies? To complete this task, follow the directions below.
1. Define four or more types or categories of movies (example: comedy, action, horror, drama, etc.).
2. Create a data retrieval chart which shows the type of movie and has a category for male and female responses.
3. Collect your data (survey a minimum of 26 people).
4. Create a graph to show your results.
5. Create a lab report to communicate your findings.
6. Share your findings with the class.
   To extend:
1. Compare the preferences at your grade level to that of another.

Task #3: The Reading Experiment

Directions: What kinds of adjectives does your favorite author use? To complete this task, follow the directions below.
1. Pick a chapter from a book you are reading.
2. On a separate sheet of paper, record all the adjectives found.
3. Look at the adjectives to find groups or reoccurring patterns.
4. Move the adjectives into groups.
5. Using tally marks, record the number of each kind of adjective.
6. Create a graph to show your results.
7. Create a lab report to communicate your findings.
8. Share your findings with the class.

1. Find a book by a different author.
2. Use the same categories to compare the adjectives found here to those of the first author.
3. Graph and share your results.

Checklist

A checklist can also be used here to rate and check off each skill required in the tasks above (Figure 11.3).

Figure 11.3 Checklist to Assess Inquiry Tasks

Checklist of Inquiry Skills

4 = outstanding, 3 = very good, 2 = average, 1 = low

Student	Skill	Teacher
	asks a question	
	collects data	
	organizes data	
	uses data to answer questions	
	uses graph or table to report data	
	writes a lab report	
	communicates findings	
	edits final product	

Student _____

Teacher _____

Grade _____

Comments:

SUMMARY

1. Scores on standardized tests can be improved by teaching test-taking strategies.
2. Performance based standards describe a set of skills to be mastered.
3. Thinking skills can be used to teach and assess performance based standards.
4. One inquiry task can be designed to teach and assess several standards.

References

Noddings, N. (1997). Thinking about standards. <u>Phi Delta Kappan, 79</u>, 184-189.

Reigeluth, C.M. (1997). Educational Standards: To standardize or to customize learning? <u>Phi Delta Kappan, 79</u>, 202-206.

Appendix

JOHNSON LESSON PLAN FORMAT

Teacher: _____ Grade: _____

Subject: _____ Time: _____

I. OBJECTIVE:

II. INTRODUCTION:

III. INPUT AND ACTIVITIES:

IV. CLOSURE:

* Use the back side for lesson reflection. What worked well? What surprised you? What would you do differently?

Criteria for Lesson Plans

Below are a set of criteria the pre-service teachers, teacher educators, and practicing teachers can use in their lesson.

CRITERIA	yes	no	sometimes
1. The lesson is fun, interesting, or informative; values students' ideas; and does not rely exclusively on closed-ended questions.			
2. The OBJECTIVE is a short, concise statement that describes exactly what students are to know or be able to do.			
3. All INPUT and ACTIVITY directly support the OBJECTIVE.			
4. The INTRODUCTION is concise and used to introduce students to concepts or material found in the lesson.			
5. The INPUT lists exactly what is taught. A reader would be able to pick up the lesson and teach this lesson. Discussion questions are written out.			
6. Information found in the INPUT is organized and logically sequenced.			
7. The lesson plan uses language and activities that are appropriate to students' developmental level.			
8. If a skill is being taught, guided instruction is used. The independent activity is practice of a skill that has been introduced and practiced in the lesson. Students are able to do the independent activity with a minimum of frustration.			
9. All lesson parts are included and clearly identified: (a) OBJECTIVE, (b) INTRODUCTION, (c) ACTIVITY, and (d) CLOSURE/REVIEW.			
10. The teacher includes reflection as a post-lesson activity.			

Smart Chart

Find an example of characters or events in the newspaper, literature, or community where the following traits are displayed:

Word Smart:

Logic or Math Smart:

Space Smart:

Body Smart:

Music Smart:

People Smart:

Nature Smart:

Other Kinds of Smart:

Skills for Cooperative Learning

	Group 1	Group 2	Group 3	Group 4	Group 5
I. FORMING SKILLS					
1. Move quickly and quietly into groups.					
2. Stay with the group.					
3. Use quiet voices.					
4. Take turns.					
II. FUNCTIONING SKILLS					
1. Share ideas and opinions.					
2. Look at the speaker.					
3. Use each other's names.					
4. Express support and acceptance.					
5. Ask for help or clarification.					
6. Energize the group.					
III. DISCUSSION SKILLS					
1. Summarize or restate.					
2. Describe feelings.					
3. Criticize ideas, not people.					
4. Ask for justification.					

Feelings Chart

Characters

Events	

Feelings Comparison Chart

Find an event from the story. Pick one character from the story. Describe that character's feelings related to the event. Then describe an event from your own life that caused similar feelings.

Story Event	*Character - Feelings*	*Your Life Event - Feeling*

T-Chart

Conclusions:

Compare-O-Graph

Web-of-Comparison

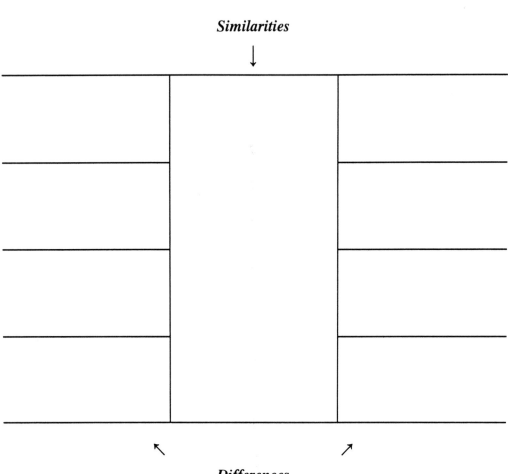

Similarities

↓

↖   ↗

Differences

Conclusions:

Infer-O-Gram

Inference Question:

What you observe	What you know

Inference:

Support a Statement

Statement	*Supporting Clues or Information*

Rating

Item:

Rating: 4 = very high, 3 = good, 2 = average, 1 = low

Critiera	Rating

Total:

Ranking

Criteria

Item	1	2	3	4	Total

Ranking: 4 = highest; 1 = lowest

Criteria
1.

2.

3.

4.

Rubrics

Task:

Levels

Criteria	3	2	1

Poem Starter

I. Topic: Start with a thought. Use semantic webbing to create a number of different ideas to find your topic.

II. Texture: Using your topic, fill in the chart below.

I hear ...	
I see ...	
I feel ...	
I taste ...	
I smell ...	
Just like ...	

DRC for Recording Behaviors.

Animal:

Behaviors

Ideas or Conclusions:

DRC for Decision-Making

Problem:

Solution	Positive Consequences	Negative Consequences

Decision:

Supporting Statements:

DRC for Ranking Decisisons

Each group member ranks the solutions 1-5, with 5 being the highest and 1 being the lowest ranking. Totals for all students' rankings are tabulated in the far right column.

Issue:

Students

Solutions					TOTAL

Decision:

Discussion Web

Yes   **No**

Question

DRC for Facts and Opinions.

Issue:

Facts	Opinions

Conclusion:

Checklist for Science Skills

Skills

___ observe	___ use data base
___ describe	___ predict
___ create a diagram	___ make groups
___ create a graph	___ ask a question
___ create a table	___ create a DRC
___ measure	___ organize data
___ record	___ demonstrate
___ use a lab report	___ conclude

I = introduced,   L = learned,   M = mastered

Creative Problem Solver

1. Problem:

2. Ideas/Solutions:

3. Best Idea/Solution (refine):

Costs of the Solution	*Benefits of the Solution*

Index

Z

NOTES

NOTES

NOTES